It's My State!

SOUTH DAKOTA
The Mount Rushmore State

Ruth Bjorklund, Geoffrey M. Horn, and Alicia Klepeis

Cavendish Square

New York

Published in 2017 by Cavendish Square Publishing, LLC
243 5th Avenue, Suite 136, New York, NY 10016

Third Edition

Website: cavendishsq.com

This publication represents the opinions and views of the author based on his or her personal experience, knowledge, and research. The information in this book serves as a general guide only. The author and publisher have used their best efforts in preparing this book and disclaim liability rising directly or indirectly from the use and application of this book.

CPSIA Compliance Information: Batch #CS16CSQ

All websites were available and accurate when this book was sent to press.

Library of Congress Cataloging-in-Publication Data
Names: Bjorklund, Ruth, author. | Horn, Geoffrey M., author. | Klepeis, Alicia, 1971- author.
Title: South Dakota / Ruth Bjorklund, Geoffrey M. Horn, and Alicia Klepeis.
Description: New York : Cavendish Square Publishing, [2016] | Series: It's my state! | Includes index. | Description based on print version record and CIP data provided by publisher; resource not viewed.
Identifiers: LCCN 2015046512 (print) | LCCN 2015046471 (ebook) | ISBN 9781627132244 (ebook) | ISBN 9781627132220 (library bound)
Subjects: LCSH: South Dakota—Juvenile literature.
Classification: LCC F651.3 (print) | LCC F651.3 .B58 2016 (ebook) | DDC 978.3—dc23
LC record available at http://lccn.loc.gov/2015046512

Editorial Director: David McNamara
Editor: Fletcher Doyle
Copy Editor: Nathan Heidelberger
Art Director: Jeffrey Talbot
Designer: Alan Sliwinski
Production Assistant: Karol Szymczuk
Photo Research: J8 Media

The photographs in this book are used by permission and through the courtesy of: welcomia/Shutterstock.com, cover; Nature PL/Superstock, USDA-NRCS PLANTS Database/Herman, D.E. et al. 1996. North Dakota tree handbook USDA NRCS ND State Soil Conservation Committee; NDSU Extension and Western Area Power Admin. Bismarck, ND/File: Picea glauca tree.jpg - Wikimedia Commons, Minden Pictures/Superstock, 4, 8, 20; Robert La Salle/Aqua-Photo/Alamy, Wikipedia Loves Art participant "The_Wookies (http://www.flickr.com/groups/wikipedia_loves_art/pool/tags/The_Wookies/)"/ File: WLA hmns Triceratops.jpg /Wikimedia Commons, Mark Newman/Superstock, 5; Navin75/Flickr: Black Hills (http://flickr.com/photos/23597588@N00/6180719727)/ File: Black Hills from Harney Peak.jpg /Wikimedia Commons, 6; Stephen Krasemann/Getty Images, 9; Westgraphix LLC, 10; MCT/Getty Images, 12; age fotostock/Superstock, 13, 18, 21, 68; Connie Ricca/Corbis, Sergio Pitamitz/Robert Harding World Imagery/Corbis, Guimir/File: Adult bison and calf, Custer State Park, South Dakota (2009-08-25).jpg/Wikimedia Commons, 14; Jeff the quiet/File: Mammoth Site Hot Springs.jpg - Wikimedia Commons, Jim Parkin/Alamy, Wkmwiki/File: WoundedKneeMuseumWallSD.jpg/ Wikimedia Commons 15; Hal Beral VWPics/Superstock, 16; Craig Lovell/Eagle Visions Photography/Alamy, 17; Belinda Images/Superstock, 19; Anthony Butera/Superstock, 20; James Hager/Robert Harding Picture Library/Superstock, Bob Wick, Bureau of Land Management (https://www.flickr.com/people/91981596@N06)/File: Greater Sage-Grouse Conservation (16759460184).jpg /Wikimedia Commons, 21; Paul Damien/National Geographic/ Getty Images, 22; Bridgeman Art Library/Superstock , 24; ClassicStock.com/Superstock, 26; AP Photo/Capital Journal, Mary Gales Askren, 28; David David Gallery/Superstock, 29; Julie Alissi/J8 Media, 30; Stock Montage/ Superstock, 31; Universal Images Group/Superstock, 32; Marilyn Angel Wynn/Getty Images, 33; Original uploader was Colin.faulkingham at en.wikipedia (http://en.wikipedia.org)/File: Sioux falls sd falls park.jpg/ Wikimedia Commons, Richard Cummins/Superstock, 34, 61; National Park Service/ http://www.nps.gov/media/photo/view.htm?id=F3CA6BF5-155D-4519-3E80B02C8EC4100F/File: Yankton and the Meridian Bridge.JPG/Wikimedia Commons, Jack Boucher (1931–2012) Library of Congress, Prints and Photograph Division HABS: SD,14-VERM,3-12 (http://hdl.loc.gov/loc.pnp/hhh.sd0008)/File: Old Main, University of South Dakota.jpg/ Wikimedia Commons, 35; Everett Collection Inc./Alamy, 36; AP Photo, 38; PJF News/Alamy, 40; Prisma/Superstock, 41; Joseph Sohm/Shutterstock.com, 44; Blaine Harrington/age fotostock/Superstock, 46; Becky Luigart-Stayner/Corbis, 47; s_bukley/Shutterstock.com, 48, 49; SuperStock/Superstock, &DC (http://www.flickr.com/people/76730958@N07) from Coulsdon, Gtr London, United Kingdom/File: Becky Hammon London 2012 Olympics Womens Basketball (Australia v Russia).jpg /Wikimedia Commons, 48; Moviestore Collections Ltd. /Alamy, AP Photo, 49; George Barille/Accurate Art, Inc., 50; Michael Matthews/Alamy, 51; HANDOUT/KRT/Newscom, 53; AP Photo/Dirk Lammers, File, 54, 59; PeopleScapes/Greg Latza, 54; Jonathan Larsen/Diadem Images/Alamy, David O. Bailey/Alamy, 55; Walter Bibikow/AWL Images/Getty Images, 56; AP Photo/Doug Dreyer, 58; Getty Images, 62, 69, 72; Hulton Archive/Getty Images, Science Faction/Superstock, 62; DKVardiman/Shutterstock.com, 64; Lyroky/Alamy, 66; imagebroker.net/Superstock, 68; Furlong Photography/Alamy, 69; Aneta_Gu/Shutterstock.com, 70; Popular Science/Getty Images, 71; Don Johnston/Superstock, 73; Christopher Santoro, 74; AP photo/Chet Brokaw, File, Jason Patrick Ross/Shutterstock.com, 75; CSQ, Universal Images Group Limited/Alamy, 76.

Printed in the United States of America

SOUTH DAKOTA
CONTENTS

A Quick Look at South Dakota...4

1. The Mount Rushmore State...7
South Dakota County Map...10
South Dakota Population by County...11
10 Key Sites...14
10 Key Plants and Animals...20

2. From the Beginning...23
The Native People...26
Making Fossils...30
10 Key Cities...34
10 Key Dates in State History...43

3. The People...45
10 Key People...48
10 Key Events...54

4. How the Government Works...57
Political Figures from South Dakota...62
You Can Make a Difference...63

5. Making a Living...65
10 Key Industries...68
Recipe for Sunflower Seed Cookies...70

South Dakota State Map...74
South Dakota Map Skills...75
State Flag, Seal, and Song...76
Glossary...77
More About South Dakota...78
Index...79

A QUICK LOOK AT

★ State Flower: American Pasque Flower

The pasque flower blooms in early spring, often before the snow melts. This pale lavender wildflower may look delicate, but it is a hardy plant common to the northern prairie and the Great Plains. The pasque flower is a member of the buttercup family. It's also known as the May Day flower.

★ State Tree: Black Hills Spruce

The Black Hills spruce is a type of evergreen. It is a cone-shaped tree with dark blue-green needles. The Black Hills region is covered with so many of these trees that the hills appear black from a distance. That's how this area got its name. These trees are sometimes used for pulpwood or as Christmas trees.

★ State Bird: Ring-Necked Pheasant

Ring-necked pheasants look like chickens with long tails. Males are brightly colored in red, gold, and green with a white ring around their necks. Females are more drab and brownish. These seed-eating birds live near wheat fields and cornfields and make their nests in the state's vast grasslands.

SOUTH DAKOTA

POPULATION: 814,180

State Fish: Walleye

The walleye is a torpedo-shaped fish that likes cold freshwater. Known for its good night vision, the fish can hunt for food in almost total darkness. South Dakotans who fish know that the best times to catch a walleye are at dawn and at dusk, when the light is dim.

State Fossil: *Triceratops*

In prehistoric times, the plant-eating *Triceratops* roamed across the region that is now the Great Plains. This dinosaur weighed as much as 6 tons (5.4 metric tons) and had a bony ruffle called a frill around its head. On its brow, it had two horns. It also had a long snout. Its name means "three-horned face."

State Animal: Coyote

Called "prairie wolves" by the explorers Meriwether Lewis and William Clark, coyotes can be found across the state. They are fast-moving creatures that live in packs. They use loud howls and playful yips to communicate with one another. Coyotes can run up to 40 miles per hour (64 kilometers per hour).

The beautiful Black Hills are part of the rugged
region of South Dakota west of the Missouri River.

The Mount Rushmore State

S outh Dakota is known as the Mount Rushmore State. If you think about this name and the state's other nicknames, the Sunshine State and the Coyote State, you still may not have a clear picture of what South Dakota is all about.

Yes, the sun shines more than two hundred days each year, but the wind blows, lightning strikes, and rain or snow falls. Coyotes do wander about the state, but they roam alongside deer, prairie dogs, and herds of pronghorns (sometimes called antelope) and bison (sometimes called buffalo). The Mount Rushmore National Memorial, with its huge sculptures of four presidents of the United States, is South Dakota's most famous tourist attraction, but the state offers much more.

South Dakota is rich in ancient history and fossil sites, traditional cultures, Old West towns, dramatic mountains, grasslands, caves, and national parks. No single nickname can really do

South Dakota Borders	
North:	North Dakota
South:	Nebraska
East:	Minnesota Iowa
West:	Montana Wyoming

South Dakota is among the best places to hunt for dinosaur bones.

justice to the state, which includes sixty-six counties and covers a land area of 75,811 square miles (196,350 square kilometers). At times, the state has been called the Land of Infinite Variety, which might be the best description of all.

Prairies, Potholes, Badlands, and Buttes

If you and three friends each lived at one of the farthest corners of the United States and wanted to meet in the country's exact middle, you would gather on a lonely piece of prairie about 17 miles (27 kilometers) west of Castle Rock, South Dakota. At the geographic center of the country, South Dakota is where east meets west.

One thing to keep in mind is that once you cross the Missouri River in South Dakota, you had better reset the time on your watch. Eastern South Dakota is in the central time zone, while western South Dakota follows mountain time.

South Dakota's landscape changes as you travel from east to west. During the last Ice Age, which began about 2.5 million years ago and ended about 11,000 years ago, huge sheets of moving ice, called glaciers, advanced and retreated over large parts of northern North America. In what is now northeastern South Dakota, glaciers shaped the landscape as they dragged rocks and **debris** across the land. The glaciers also created hills pitted with small lakes and ponds called "prairie potholes." In 1839, French mapmaker Joseph Nicollet described the area as "beautiful to the eyes." Today, hawks, eagles, owls, ducks, and hundreds of other birds continue to flock to these bodies of water. Trees such as maple, ironwood, chokecherry, and box elder thrive in the area, as well as wildflowers of almost every color.

In southeastern South Dakota, tall prairie grasses added nutrients to the soil for more than ten thousand years. Today, much of this land is used for farming, and rolling fields of corn, soybeans, oats, and wheat extend as far as the eye can see. Much of South Dakota's population lives in the eastern part of the state, in cities such as Sioux Falls and Brookings,

The prairie lands of eastern South Dakota are home to a lot of wildlife, including coyotes.

Night Sky Viewing

With very few buildings and almost no light pollution in the area, the Badlands are one of the best places in the country to go stargazing. Looking at the night sky here, it's not uncommon to see up to 7,500 stars—and a clear view of the Milky Way Galaxy—with the naked eye.

or on nearby farms. Rivers and streams flow through the region. Willow and cottonwood trees line the banks of many of the rivers and streams. Pheasants, waterfowl, and deer make their homes among these trees.

The Missouri River, known as the Big Muddy, flows from north to south through South Dakota, dividing the state nearly in half. For centuries, the constantly shifting river was the heart of a huge valley. It was filled with vast herds of bison, as well as with bears, elk, wolves, bighorn sheep, whooping cranes, and other wildlife. As Lakota Sioux John Fire Lame Deer said, "Animals are part of us. [T]he winged and four-legged are our cousins … There is power in the buffalo. There is power in the antelope. There was great power in a wolf, even in a coyote. To us, life, all life, is sacred."

Today, dams built to improve agriculture and commerce have turned the Missouri River into a series of four large lakes, or reservoirs. Little of the river has been left to run wild, and little of the original wildlife remains. Blackbirds, flickers, and pheasants can still be seen in this region, however, along with ducks, geese, deer, and coyotes.

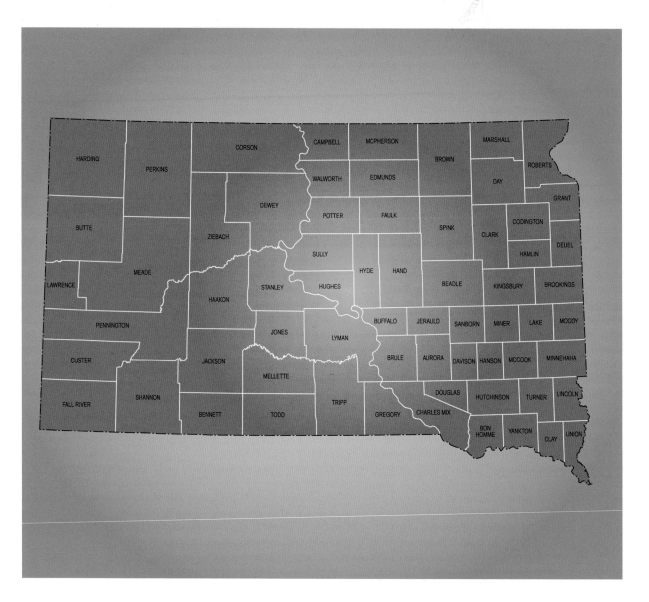

SOUTH DAKOTA
POPULATION BY COUNTY

County	Population	County	Population	County	Population
Aurora County	2,710	Grant County	7,356	Minnehaha County	169,468
Beadle County	17,398	Gregory County	4,271	Moody County	6,486
Bennett County	3,431	Haakon County	1,937	Pennington County	100,948
Bon Homme County	7,070	Hamlin County	5,903	Perkins County	2,982
Brookings County	31,965	Hand County	3,431	Potter County	2,329
Brown County	36,531	Hanson County	3,331	Roberts County	10,149
Brule County	5,255	Harding County	1,255	Sanborn County	2,355
Buffalo County	1,912	Hughes County	17,022	Shannon County	13,586
Butte County	10,110	Hutchinson County	7,343	Spink County	6,415
Campbell County	1,466	Hyde County	1,420	Stanley County	2,966
Charles Mix County	9,129	Jackson County	3,031	Sully County	1,373
Clark County	3,691	Jerauld County	2,071	Todd County	9,612
Clay County	13,864	Jones County	1,006	Tripp County	5,644
Codington County	27,227	Kingsbury County	5,148	Turner County	8,347
Corson County	4,050	Lake County	11,200	Union County	14,399
Custer County	8,216	Lawrence County	24,097	Walworth County	5,438
Davison County	19,504	Lincoln County	44,828	Yankton County	22,438
Day County	5,710	Lyman County	3,755	Ziebach County	2,801
Deuel County	4,363	Marshall County	4,656		
Dewey County	5,301	McCook County	5,618		
Douglas County	3,002	McPherson County	2,459		
Edmunds County	4,071	Meade County	25,434		
Fall River County	7,094	Melette County	2,048		
Faulk County	2,364	Miner County	2,389		

Source: US Bureau of the Census, 2010

The Gavins Point Dam near Yankton turns the mighty Missouri River into hydroelectric power.

In what is now the state of South Dakota, Ice Age glaciers did not spread west of the Missouri River. More than seventy million years ago, western South Dakota was the floor of an ancient sea. Layers of rock, clay, sand, silt, and other debris settled there. Over time, as the sea dried up, wind and water wore down the layers into different shapes. These layers contain an important record of prehistoric life, making South Dakota one of the best places to study fossils.

More than ten thousand bones were found at the site known as the Big Pig Dig in Badlands National Park, where the remains of ancient horses, dogs, saber-toothed cats, rhinoceroses, and deer were uncovered. Two visitors to the park discovered the Big Pig Dig fossil bed in 1993. During the next fifteen years, the site attracted more than five thousand visitors every summer. The dig officially ended in 2008, but scientists have continued to study the fossils that were found there.

West of the Missouri River, the land rises and becomes drier. The region is also less populated than eastern South Dakota. In the western part of the state, there are ranches and a few remote farms. Short grasses such as blue grama and buffalo grass sprout for miles in much of western South Dakota. Farther west, sharp **spires** of rock and clay form a geographic region known as the Badlands. In 1839, a Catholic missionary,

Badlands National Park covers 244,000 acres (99,000 hectares).

Pierre-Jean De Smet, wrote that the Badlands, from a distance, looked like "ancient castles." Folded, twisted, and difficult to travel through, the Badlands are covered in brush and grass, prickly pear cactus, yucca, and sage. The region is home to many creatures, such as rattlesnakes, eagles, prairie dogs, rabbits, pronghorns, and bison.

Much of the soil west of the Missouri River is a hard, red adobe clay called gumbo. When it rains, gumbo clay becomes slick and gooey. Most country roads are made of this sticky mixture, and smart locals know when and how to avoid getting stuck. However, gumbo is hardly the only kind of soil in the Coyote State. South Dakota has more than five hundred different kinds of soil. In 1990, Houdek soil was chosen as the official state soil. Very deep and well drained, Houdek soil gets its dark surface color from decayed plants and other materials deposited over thousands of years.

Southwest of the Badlands region is another South Dakota natural treasure—the Black Hills. These ancient mountains were formed from magma, or hot liquid rock, that came out of ancient volcanoes close to one billion years ago. This magma then cooled and hardened. The Black Hills, sacred to the area's Native Americans, are ninety million years older than the Rocky Mountains. The Lakota Sioux named them Paha Sapa, which means "hills that are black."

Giant granite peaks and deep canyons add to the beauty of the Black Hills. Trees such as oak, ash, willow, and aspen can be found there. The region also holds a wealth

Corn Palace

Crazy Horse Memorial

Custer State Park

1. Badlands National Park

This park's bizarre rock formations are the result of **erosion**. The mixed-grass prairie is home to bison, bighorn sheep, prairie dogs, and other animals. Some of the world's richest fossil beds rest in the park's 244,000 acres (98,743 hectares).

2. Black Hills National Forest

Located in western South Dakota (and northeast Wyoming), this forest features deep blue lakes, rugged rock formations, canyons, and more than 1,300 miles (2,092 km) of streams. Biking, hiking, horseback riding, and fishing are some of the activities available.

3. Corn Palace

Described by some as the "agricultural show-place of the world," Mitchell's Corn Palace has been around for more than 120 years. Each year, its incredibly detailed murals are completely redone with a new theme, using thirteen colors/shades of corn.

4. Crazy Horse Memorial

Dedicated to the Oglala Lakota Sioux warrior Crazy Horse, this mountain sculpture has been under construction since 1948. Visitors to the memorial can check out a model of what the memorial, which will eventually stand 563 feet (173 meters) tall, will look like when completed.

5. Custer State Park

Custer State Park is South Dakota's oldest and largest state park. Located in the Black Hills town of Custer, this park offers scenic drives, chuck wagon cookouts, and great trout fishing.

SOUTH DAKOTA

6. Ingalls Homestead

Visitors can go back in time when visiting the homestead of author Laura Ingalls Wilder, who settled in De Smet with her family in the 1880s. Drive a covered wagon or go to school in a one-room schoolhouse at this historical site.

7. The Mammoth Site

Located in Hot Springs, this active **paleontological** dig site contains the world's largest concentration of mammoth remains. Visitors can see a working paleontology lab and check out some of the world's best Ice Age fossils. Kids can even dig for mammoth remains.

The Mammoth Site

8. Mount Rushmore National Memorial

Gutzon Borglum's enormous sculpture, located near Keystone, is one of the most famous symbols of America. The faces of four US presidents are carved into the South Dakotan granite: George Washington, Abraham Lincoln, Thomas Jefferson, and Theodore Roosevelt.

Mount Rushmore National Memorial

9. Wind Cave National Park

Established in 1903 in Hot Springs, Wind Cave is one of the United States' earliest national parks. Tourists can hike above ground or take tours to explore the extensive underground caverns. The Sioux people consider this cave to be sacred.

10. Wounded Knee Museum

The exhibits allow visitors to follow a path through the December 1890 Wounded Knee Massacre, when up to three hundred Lakota people were killed by US troops. Other exhibits focus on pre-Columbian America and South Dakotan culture.

Wounded Knee Museum

Mountain goats are not native to South Dakota but have lived in the state for nearly one hundred years.

of wildflowers, including prairie coneflowers, black-eyed Susans, larkspurs, lady's slippers, and primrose. Deer, wild turkeys, and elk live in the woodlands. The high ridges and lush meadows nearby are home to bison, golden and bald eagles, coyotes, beavers, porcupines, prairie dogs, bobcats, and mountain lions. About two hundred mountain goats roam the Black Hills. Some of them can be traced back to six goats that were given by Canada to Custer State Park in 1924. The goats escaped from their pens and made their homes amid the region's rugged peaks. The population reached as high as four hundred before it started to decline rapidly in 2000. Recently, goats from Colorado and Utah have been added to the herd to boost its numbers.

Some of the wonders of this region are below the ground. Limestone caves line the area, complete with cone-shaped rock formations and frost crystals. The Black Hills region is known for its many caves. Probably the most famous of these caves can be visited at Wind Cave National Park. Here visitors can see formations that look like honeycomb and others that resemble popcorn. There is also a formation known as frostwork, which gets its name from the way it appears much like a small bush covered with frost.

Prairie Wildlife

The fossil sites throughout the state show that the prairie has long been home to a wide variety of creatures. From the large meat-eating dinosaur *Tyrannosaurus rex* to the present-day coyote, wildlife has thrived in South Dakota's prairie potholes, rivers, and grasslands, as well as in the Badlands and the Black Hills.

In 1804, explorer Meriwether Lewis climbed a hill along the Missouri River. He wrote that as he looked below, he saw bison, elk, and deer "feeding in every direction." Together with his fellow explorer William Clark, Lewis took note of hundreds of grassland animals living on America's prairies. The land had animals such as grizzly bears, bison, prairie dogs, bighorn sheep, coyotes, prairie chickens, and black-footed ferrets. The settlers who later came to farm the plains drove many of these creatures away.

The largest and most complete *Tyrannosaurus rex* skeleton ever found is named for Sue Hendrickson, who discovered the bones near Faith.

It's impossible to talk about the state of South Dakota without mentioning bison. The scientific name for the large, ox-like mammals that formerly flourished in the American West is *Bison bison*. Many people call these animals either "buffalo" or "American buffalo," but scientists prefer the term "bison." They reserve the name "buffalo" for species (types of animals) that are not found in North America.

At one time, seventy million bison roamed the prairie. By 1883, the bison was nearly extinct (that is, they had almost completely died out) due to overhunting. Today, there are herds of bison at Wind Cave and Badlands National Parks, Custer State Park, Buffalo Gap National Grasslands, Black Hills National Forest, and several private ranches. About 1,300 bison roam freely through Custer State Park. They make up one of the largest publicly owned bison herds in the world.

Environmental Protection

At the time Lewis and Clark passed through what is now South Dakota, much of the land was covered by prairie dog towns. Prairie dogs loosen the soil when they dig their underground tunnels. Farmers thought the animals were pests and, over time, tried to rid the land of them. In doing so, however, they also harmed the black-footed ferret, which lived in prairie dog towns and hunted prairie dogs at night. Because the ferret's food source had shrunk, experts thought the ferrets had disappeared. Then one day in 1981, a rancher's dog returned home with a black-footed ferret it had caught. Some had survived. Today, this clever hunter is on the federal government's endangered species list. (An animal considered endangered is at risk of becoming extinct.) National Forest Service and National Park Service workers have brought black-footed ferrets into protected prairie dog towns in Badlands National Park and Buffalo Gap National Grasslands.

For ages, hundreds of species of birds and ducks have made their nests in the prairie wetlands. However, in the past century, most of the wetlands have been changed into farmland. Concerned citizens and government agencies are working to preserve the remaining wetlands for future generations of teal, cormorants, grebes, Canada and snow

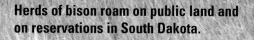

Herds of bison roam on public land and on reservations in South Dakota.

geese, pelicans, herons, cranes, swans, hawks, and eagles. Wildlife **refuges** have been set up, and many farmers have agreed not to disturb nests or pools of standing water until after the mating season. By working together, park rangers, environmentalists, and the concerned citizens of South Dakota are helping to protect and preserve many of North America's native animals.

Climate

The seasons differ sharply in South Dakota. In 1936, for example, temperatures went from a winter low of –58 degrees Fahrenheit (–50 degrees Celsius) to a summer high of 120°F (49°C). That was a difference of 178°F (99°C) in the same year. In summer, temperatures average 70°F (21°C), but highs during the day of 100°F (38°C) or more are fairly common. Humidity, or moisture in the air, is generally low, so residents claim that the dry summer heat is bearable. Spring and fall feature pleasant temperatures.

Summer thunderstorms can be violent, come up quickly, and produce many lightning strikes.

Winter blizzards blast residents with fierce winds, blinding snow, and arctic temperatures. On average, 18 inches (46 centimeters) of precipitation fall each year. Precipitation is measured as the amount of rain plus the amount of water in melted snow. Powdery snow contains little precipitation. The northwest receives about 14 inches (36 cm). Approximately 25 inches (64 cm) fall in the southeast. Most precipitation in South Dakota falls as rain; Sioux Falls receives an average annual snowfall of 44.5 inches (113 cm). In spring, the rains can come hard and often, flooding the plains and damaging homes, towns, crops, and roadways. In the winter and early spring, South Dakota can be affected by chinook winds. These warm, dry winds blow along the Rocky Mountains, warming as they move east to lower elevations. On January 22, 1943, windows in the town of Spearfish broke when a chinook wind caused the temperature to rise 49°F (27°C) in just two minutes. At 7:30 a.m., the temperature was an icy –4°F (–20°C), but by 7:32, it was 45°F (7°C).

In the summer, thunderstorms are sudden and often violent. They can carry harmful hail, heavy rain, lightning, and wind gusts of 50 to 100 miles per hour (80 to 160 kilometers per hour). According to the National Weather Service office in Sioux Falls, a single prairie thunderstorm can deliver fifty thousand lightning strikes.

Coneflower

Cottonwood Tree

Golden Eagle

1. Bison

In the days before white settlers arrived, millions of wild bison occupied South Dakota's plains. They were hunted almost to the point of extinction, but their numbers have grown. Small bison herds now live in South Dakota's state and national parks.

2. Buffalo Grass

Buffalo grass has short stems and grows all over the Great Plains. Native peoples used the grass for basket weaving and its berries for dye. Early settlers used the sod it provided to make their homes. Today, it's still a favorite food of bison.

3. Coneflower

Purple and yellow coneflowers grow well in the prairie's extreme climate. Native Americans used the roots of this plant to make a tea to cure sore throats, snakebites, and colds. The popular remedy known as echinacea (eck-uh-NAY-sha) comes from purple coneflowers.

4. Cottonwood Tree

Cottonwood trees, with their puffy white seeds and shimmering leaves, were a welcome sight for pioneers. On the mostly treeless planes, they provided shade, timber, and fuel for cooking, and they indicated water was nearby.

5. Golden Eagle

Golden eagles are large birds of prey with gold feathers on their heads, sharp talons, and hooked beaks. They use their huge eyes to spot prey. A golden eagle can spy a rabbit from more than 1 mile (1.6 km) away.

6. Prairie Dog

These small mammals often make their homes underground in South Dakota's grassland areas. Living in most of the western two-thirds of the state, prairie dogs have a stable population. People even get licenses to hunt these furry, highly social animals.

7. Prairie Rose

Often picked for its wonderful scent, this flower has five pink petals with a yellow center. Some people call this native plant a "meadow rose" or "smooth rose." The USDA considers it a weed!

8. Pronghorn

For more than one million years, pronghorns have roamed the Great Plains. These mammals can run at speeds up to 60 miles per hour (97 kmh). After being overhunted in the nineteenth century, conservation efforts have restored its population to nearly eight hundred thousand.

9. Sage Grouse

The largest of the North American grouse, sage grouse are native to the sagebrush flats in northwestern South Dakota. Mature grouse eat sage leaves and use sage as cover. Elimination of sage plants has led to declining populations.

10. Western Hognose Snake

The western hognose snake is also known as the puff adder or hissing adder. Though it hisses when frightened, the hognose isn't venomous. The hognose hunts for prey like salamanders and insects by using its pointed snout to dig in the dirt.

Praire Dog

Pronghorn

Sage Grouse

Mammoth bones are among the many discoveries made by paleontologists near Hot Springs.

From the Beginning

You can see the passage of time in the land we know as South Dakota. From sixty-five million years ago, when dinosaurs such as *Tyrannosaurus rex* ruled the land, to the recent past, when the bones of a *T. rex* nicknamed Sue were discovered, the state has taken a dramatic march through the ages.

The First People

The first humans known to have entered the South Dakota region are called Paleo-Indians. "Paleo" means ancient. It is believed they arrived more than ten thousand years ago, after their ancestors crossed a land bridge from Asia into North America. (The land bridge, which existed because sea levels were lower before the glaciers of the Ice Age melted, is now underwater.) The Paleo-Indians were following bison (larger ancestors of present-day bison), ground sloths, mammoths, and other large mammals. They hunted these animals using spears with sharp stone points. When the climate changed, the larger animals died off. The Paleo-Indians then turned to fishing, hunting smaller creatures, and gathering nuts and berries.

People known as Mound Builders followed the Paleo-Indians and began to move into what is now eastern South Dakota about 1,500 years ago. These people are called Mound

Builders because they formed large mounds of dirt to bury and honor their dead. Like the Paleo-Indians, the Mound Builders fished, hunted small game, and gathered nuts and berries. They also farmed the land, growing crops including beans, maize (corn), and squash. They tended to build and settle in small villages along the rivers such as the Missouri and the Big Sioux River. These villages were year-round settlements. **Archaeologists** who have studied the Mound Builder sites in South Dakota have found ancient pottery, stone tools, flint arrowpoints, and decorative beads made from shells. Hunters began using the bow and arrow around the time of the Mound Builders.

Allies and Enemies

Sometime between the fourteenth and sixteenth centuries, the Native American group known as the Arikara people followed the Missouri River north into what is now South Dakota. The river was the center of the Arikaras' lives. They used the river's high bluffs for their earth lodge villages. They also took advantage of the rich soil near the river for their gardens. The Arikara women planted and tended these gardens. They grew a variety of crops, including corn, squash, beans, tobacco, and sunflowers. During the summer and

The Sioux became expert bison hunters after learning to ride horses.

late fall, the Arikara people went bison hunting. These Native Americans were successful villagers, traders, and farmers. Nomadic tribes such as the Cheyenne, Pawnee, and Crow also moved into the area. The Arikaras traded their horses and extra food to the nomadic tribes for bison meat, skins, and fur robes.

To the east, in the region now known as Minnesota, French fur trappers and traders lived among the Ojibwe (or Chippewa) people. The French traded guns and tools to the Ojibwe for beaver pelts. The guns gave the Ojibwe power over their Native American enemies, mainly the Dakota. The Ojibwe called the Dakota "Natōwēssiwak," meaning "Little Snakes." The French translated that to "Nadouéssioux," and shortened the name to Sioux. The Dakota were forced west. They soon divided into three groups: the group that was still called the Dakota Sioux stayed in what is now western Minnesota, the Nakota Sioux settled in present-day eastern South Dakota, and the Lakota went west beyond the Missouri River.

In Ojibwe territory, the Sioux had been woodland dwellers who hunted only small animals and collected nuts and berries. Once the Sioux began living in Arikara territory, however, they learned about horses. This changed their way of life. After mastering the horse, the Sioux became skilled bison hunters and expert warriors. They also started living in portable homes called tepees. These cone-shaped dwellings were made of long wooden poles covered with animal hides. The Sioux built their tepees at a slight angle. Because of the angle, the homes could catch cool breezes in the summer. In the winter, the tepees could be turned away from the cold winds. The Sioux took pride in their tepees and often painted them with religious symbols.

The First Europeans

The first Europeans known to explore the region that is now South Dakota were two French-Canadian brothers, François and Louis-Joseph Gaultier de La Vérendrye. In 1743, they were the leaders of a small exploring party that came south from present-day Canada. These brothers claimed the territory for the king of France and inscribed their names on a

The Native People

Native people lived in the territory that is now South Dakota many thousands of years before European settlers arrived. A number of scientists believe that the Native Americans first arrived here between ten thousand and twelve thousand years ago. Many of these early residents were mainly hunters. They often used stone-tipped spears that were very sharp to kill their prey, which included mammoths, sloths, mastodons, and other mammals. People from the Arikara, Cheyenne, Ponca, and Sioux tribes were just some of the Native Americans here when European settlers came to the area now called South Dakota.

South Dakota's early Native American tribes had some traits in common with each other. The men spent lots of their time hunting for food and trading goods with other tribes. Bison were essential to the Native Americans' lives. They ate the bison meat and made soup from the blood. They used the animal hides for clothing and to build their portable homes called tepees. The Sioux were excellent horsemen and warriors. The Dakotas raised corn. Most Nakotas lived in permanent villages, unlike the nomadic Lakotas who followed bison herds. Various tribes, including all the Sioux, expanded their diet by gathering and eating nuts and wild berries.

The tepee allowed the Sioux to move easily from place to place in search of food.

After the Europeans arrived, the lives of South Dakota's Native Americans changed. In the eighteenth century, Europeans brought diseases including smallpox to North America. The Native Americans did not have resistance to such diseases. Many thousands of Arikara and other Native American people died from European diseases. But not all European-Native American relations were bad. There were some friendly relations and trading transactions between the newly arrived settlers and the Native Americans during the early

1800s. Tensions grew as more white settlers arrived, however. This tension often had to do with Europeans interfering with Native Americans' ways of life and hunting grounds.

Today, nine federally recognized Native American tribes live in South Dakota. Eight of these tribes are Sioux and one is the Sisseton Wahpeton Oyate. About 71,800 Native Americans live in South Dakota. Many of these Native Americans live on reservations, located throughout the state.

Spotlight on the Oglala Sioux

"Sioux" is pronounced "soo." It originally comes from a French word "Nadouéssioux" (taken from an Ojibwe word), meaning "little snakes." The Oglala Sioux were known as brave warriors and excellent bison hunters among the Plains Native Americans.

Distribution: Today, many Oglala Sioux occupy the Pine Ridge Reservation, with over 2.8 million acres (1.1 million ha.). The group has around thirty-eight thousand members in South Dakota, and their main communities are in Pine Ridge, Kyle, and Wanblee.

Homes: Traditionally, the Oglala Sioux lived in moveable, cone-shaped homes called tepees (or tipis). These were typically made from bison hides and wooden poles. They used bison hides for bedding, seating, and covers inside their homes.

Food: The Oglala Sioux ate meat from whatever animals they could hunt, such as bison, deer, and elk. They supplemented this meat with roots and wild vegetables including spinach and prairie turnips. They also gathered wild berries and fruits whenever possible. If food was scarce, the Oglala Sioux would eat dried bison meat.

Clothing: Oglala Sioux men and women wore clothes made of softened deerskin or bison skin. They also wore soft leather moccasins on their feet. Women typically wore knee-length dresses with leggings underneath. Men wore leggings, tunics or shirts, and breechcloths. They sometimes used paint, porcupine quills, and beadwork to decorate their clothing.

Art: The Oglala Sioux, like many other Native American peoples in the region, created beautiful beadwork. Sometimes the beads were used to decorate clothing and moccasins. They sometimes decorated their tepees with paintings featuring geometric designs or animals.

lead plate that they buried at the top of a hill. (Amazingly, this plate lay undiscovered for 170 years. It was found in 1913 by a group of schoolchildren, who saw a small part of the plate sticking up above the ground and dug it up. Today, the Vérendrye plate is displayed at the Museum of the South Dakota State Historical Society in the city of Pierre.)

Few other Europeans came to what is now South Dakota during the eighteenth century. For the most part, Native American cultures continued to thrive, and the supply of bison for food remained plentiful. However, some of the area's Native American people suffered as the result of their early interactions with Europeans. One devastating example concerns the Arikara people. At the group's height during the eighteenth century, there were about thirty thousand Arikara people. They didn't have any natural defenses to the diseases that the European explorers brought, however. In 1780–1781, the Arikaras were nearly wiped out by a deadly smallpox **epidemic**. As interactions between Native peoples and Europeans continued, disease was a problem that plagued the Native Americans living in what is now South Dakota.

The plains were part of an area west of the Mississippi River known as the Louisiana Territory. France claimed the territory for most of the eighteenth century and in the early nineteenth century. In 1803, while Thomas Jefferson was president, the United States bought the territory from France, and the land became known as the Louisiana Purchase. This purchase doubled the size of the young American nation. Right away, President Jefferson commissioned two former military officers, Meriwether Lewis and William Clark, to explore the new land. In 1804, Lewis and Clark and their party traveled up the Missouri River through present-day South Dakota. They visited several Native American villages and camps. For the most part, their meetings were friendly.

In 1817, fur trader Joseph La Framboise established the first permanent white settlement in the region, near the present-day city of Fort Pierre. Other trappers and traders soon followed. In 1831, the *Yellowstone* made the first steamboat voyage up the Missouri River into the South Dakota region. It carried trappers and supplies into the wilderness, and it later transported furs out of the area to eastern markets. The trappers'

In Their Own Words

"I learned more about the economy from one South Dakota dust storm than I did in all my years of college."
—Hubert H. Humphrey

Lewis and Clark arrived in the area that is now South Dakota in 1804.

Making Fossils

South Dakota is a state rich in fossils. Some of the world's greatest dinosaur and mammoth fossils have been found in the state. You can make your own fossils, including items such as seashells, sticks, or even plastic animals and bugs.

What You Need

A shoebox

A package of plaster of Paris, available in
    craft stores

Sand

Squirt bottle for water

Objects such as seashells, twigs, stones,
    toy animals or bugs

Plastic knife or spoon

Toothbrush (can be an old one)

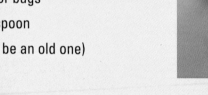

What To Do

- Place a layer of sand (about 0.5 inches or 1.25 cm deep) into your shoebox. Very lightly dampen the sand with water, using your squirt bottle. This will help create the imprint of whatever objects you press into the sand.

- Firmly press your selected objects—sticks, seashells, toy animals, etc.—into the damp sand in your shoebox. Remove these objects from the sand as carefully as you can so that their impressions are left behind.

- Following the directions on the package, mix up a batch of the plaster of Paris.

- Plaster of Paris dries quickly, so you'll want to quickly pour it over the damp sand in your shoebox. Try to cover the sand as evenly as you can. Ideally, you want the layer of plaster of Paris to be at least 0.5 inches (1.25 cm) thick.

- Using the back of the plastic spoon or a plastic knife, gently smooth out the plaster of Paris.

- After the plaster of Paris has dried, tear the shoebox away from it. Using a toothbrush, carefully brush away the excess sand from your fossil.

Sitting Bull tried to keep settlers from taking land from the Sioux.

interest in the area ended by the mid-1800s, however, once most of the beavers were gone.

As the trappers moved on, farmers from the eastern United States came to the region in search of land. The new settlers were taking over and farming Native American land, angering many Native American leaders. The newcomers also killed nearly all the bison. This cut the Native American people off from their greatest source of food, clothing, and shelter. The Native Americans were unwilling to give up their land and way of life without a fight.

The clashes between Native Americans and settlers persuaded many pioneers to turn back, but the US government wanted white people to settle the newly named Dakota Territory. US officials and Sioux leaders agreed to the Fort Laramie Treaty of 1868, which established the Great Sioux Reservation on land west of the Missouri River. The reservation included the Black Hills, a region the Sioux regarded as sacred. The treaty prohibited white folks from entering the reservation land. In exchange, the Sioux agreed to end their war against white settlers.

The treaty failed to achieve peace. As white settlers continued to travel through the overland trails of the Dakota Territory, crossing Native American land, Sioux leaders such as Crazy Horse and Sitting Bull tried to resist their advances. Red Cloud, a Lakota chief, led many battles against white settlers entering the Black Hills. He declared, "We did not ask you white men to come here. The Great Spirit gave us this country as a home. You had yours."

Calamity Jane, born Martha Jane Cannary, was a frontier scout, sharpshooter, and performer in Wild West shows.

In 1874, relations between white people and Native Americans reached a boiling point after a military officer, George Armstrong Custer, led an expedition that found gold in the Black Hills. A gold rush quickly developed, and gold seekers from across the continent arrived with hopes of getting rich. Almost overnight, the rough-and-tumble Black Hills mining towns of Deadwood and Lead became magnets for adventurers, including Calamity Jane, Wild Bill Hickok, and the famous African-American cowboy Nat Love, also known as Deadwood Dick.

Most Native Americans in the area were not pleased. After all, miners kept pouring into their lands, even though the Great Sioux Reservation belonged to the Native American people. The Sioux wanted to protect their sacred lands, but the US government had a different vision for land use. The US government wanted the Native Americans to sell off their land so it could be used for mining. The Sioux were told that the government would cut off their food supply if they did not agree to sell their Black Hills holdings. This is what's known as a "sell or starve" policy. When many Sioux still refused to sell, the government went ahead and seized control of the territory. Red Cloud described the government's actions: "They made us many promises, more than I can remember, but they never kept but one; they promised to take our land, and they took it."

Year by year, the government seized more Native American land. Some Native Americans tried to resist, but they were overpowered by government troops. At Wounded Knee Creek on the Pine Ridge Reservation, in December 1890, US Cavalry troops surrounded a cold, hungry, and lightly armed band of Native Americans. When a shot rang out, the soldiers responded with gun and cannon fire that killed hundreds of men, women, and children (mostly Sioux people). This **massacre** was the final chapter in the war between the Native Americans from the plains and the US government. As Black Elk, a Lakota holy man, lamented, "A people's dream died there."

Carving the Frontier

Eager to expand the nation, the US government had passed the Homestead Act in 1862. This act of Congress offered 160 acres (65 ha) of land in the West to any person willing to pay a small filing fee and to live and work on the land for five years. The nation was growing and changing. Railroads were being built. To speed their progress, railroad officials advertised heavily in Europe. They posted flyers that promised, "Best Wheat Lands, Best Farming Lands, Best Grazing Lands in the world … FREE TO ALL!" Soon Swedes, Germans, Russians, Czechs, Norwegians, and Danes were joining the ranks of the pioneers headed for the Dakota Territory.

Often, the first task for these pioneers was to build a house. The plains had few trees for lumber, so the farmers were forced to build their homes with hard-packed pieces of

Sod homes and carriages are among the artifacts of frontier life that can be seen at Homestead National Monument.

1. **Sioux Falls: population 153,888**

South Dakota's biggest city is a cultural and entertainment center. Visitors can experience the habitat of more than eight hundred free-flying butterflies at the Sertoma Butterfly House or view local and national **indigenous** artworks at the Prairie Star Gallery.

2. **Rapid City: population 67,956**

Rapid City features the state's largest movie theater screen and dozens of restaurants. A series of bronze life-size statues of America's presidents dot the city's sidewalks. Canyon Lake Park is great for paddle-boating.

3. **Aberdeen: population 26,091**

Voted one of the top one hundred best places to live by Livability in 2016, Aberdeen offers many outdoor activities from ice skating in winter to golfing in summer. The city's South Dakota Film Festival draws hundreds of movie buffs annually.

4. **Brookings: population 22,056**

Brookings is home to South Dakota State University. Among Its attractions are the Dakota Nature Park and Larson Nature Center, with its 135 acres (55 hectares) for hiking, biking, and kayaking, and the Children's Museum of South Dakota.

5. **Watertown: population 21,482**

Sitting between Lake Kampeska and Lake Pelican, Watertown has more than thirty-five parks. The city is also home to the Bramble Park Zoo with residents ranging from Amur tigers to red kangaroos. Redlin Art Center houses paintings by local artist Terry Redlin.

Sioux Falls

Rapid City

6. Mitchell: population 15,254

In addition to its Corn Palace, Mitchell is home to several attractions. At the Prehistoric Indian Village, there is an earth lodge like the Native Americans here would have lived in more than one thousand years ago.

7. Yankton: population 14,454

Located on the Missouri River, Yankton is a water lover's paradise. The Missouri National Recreational River runs along the city's waterfront area with miles of trails for biking and hiking, as well as a beautiful area for paddling.

8. Pierre: population 13,646

Located at nearly the geographic center of the state, Pierre is South Dakota's capital. The city features many museums, including the Verendrye Museum with its pioneer relics. The Lewis and Clark Family Center offers hands-on history lessons.

9. Huron: population 12,592

The town was settled in 1880. It is now the site of the annual South Dakota State Fair and the home of many famous people, including former vice president Hubert H. Humphrey and Gladys Pyle, the first female member of the House of Representatives.

10. Vermillion: population 10,571

Home to the state's oldest university, the University of South Dakota, Vermillion has a rich history. Lewis and Clark arrived in 1804. Vermillion's world-class National Music Museum contains over fourteen thousand instruments from around the globe.

Yankton

Vermillion

Mount Rushmore took more than fourteen years to carve.

earth called sod. They plowed the heavy top layer of sod in long strips that they cut into building blocks. Whole families stacked the heavy sod blocks on top of one another, making walls and leaving openings for windows and a door. These houses were called soddies. They stayed warm in winter and cool in summer because of the dirt roofs and walls. They were not perfect homes by any means. Many irritations came through the walls—rain, dust, snakes, rodents, and even an occasional cow walking across a low-lying roof.

Farming the plains was not a simple task. Drought was a constant threat, as were storms, prairie fires, frost, and destructive pests such as grasshoppers. Most homesteaders left their claims and moved on. Rose Wilder Lane, who lived in De Smet, South Dakota, in the late nineteenth century, wrote: "It was a saying in the Dakotas that the Government bet … that the land would starve a man out in less than five years. My father won that bet. It took seven successive years of complete crop failure … to dislodge us from that land."

Statehood

Despite the hardships, the population of the South Dakota region expanded from 11,776 in 1870 to 98,268 in 1880 and nearly 330,000 in 1889. Residents of the Dakotas believed statehood would give them pride, identity, government jobs, and other benefits. In February 1889, shortly before he left office, President Grover Cleveland signed documents formally dividing the Dakota Territory into North Dakota and South Dakota. On

Milkweed Collection

During World War II, South Dakotan school children gathered milkweed pods along the road ditches in thirty-six counties east of the Missouri River. These pods contained material that was used to provide insulation for pilots' jackets in the days before synthetic insulation was available.

November 2, 1889, President Benjamin Harrison signed the proclamation that made North Dakota and South Dakota the thirty-ninth and fortieth US states. Pierre was named South Dakota's capital because it was the closest town to the geographic center of the state.

Statehood brought little change to the day-to-day lives of South Dakotans. The state remained a difficult place to make a living, but a decade or so into the twentieth century, fortunes changed. During most of the time between 1910 and the end of World War I (which lasted from 1914 to 1918), weather was good and crops thrived. When the United States entered the war in 1917, some thirty-two thousand South Dakotans answered the government's call to join the military. Others stayed home on the farm, raising wheat, corn, and livestock to feed the rest of the nation. Patriotic posters encouraged farmers to "Sow the Seeds of Victory!"

After helping to win the war, and with enthusiasm still high, South Dakotans decided to build a monument that would attract visitors and tourist dollars to the state. They turned to a sculptor named Gutzon Borglum, who chose a granite mountain in the Black Hills on which to carve a memorial to the nation. He drew up plans to blast the granite of Mount Rushmore and carve in stone the faces of Presidents George Washington, Thomas Jefferson, Abraham Lincoln, and Theodore Roosevelt. In August 1927, President Calvin Coolidge declared the sculpture would be "a picture of hope fulfilled." Work on Mount Rushmore began on October 4, 1927, and was completed on October 31, 1941. The entire project took about four hundred workers more than fourteen years and cost $989,992.32. Each year, nearly three million visitors from the United States and around the world come to marvel at the Mount Rushmore National Memorial.

Dusty Old Dust

South Dakotans were no strangers to either success or extreme hardship. Hopeful miners gave their claims upbeat names such as "Golden Slipper Mine" or "Jackpot Mine," while other names such as "Dead Broke Mine" or "Hardscrabble Mine" told a different story. Farmers also experienced a mixture of boom and bust. In their eagerness to supply the

High winds blew dry soil that blanketed farms and towns during the Great Depression.

Black Blizzards

Experts have estimated that 850 million tons [771 million t] of topsoil vanished with the winds in 1935 during the Dust Bowl era. Huge clouds of dust, known as "black blizzards," blew through South Dakota and many other Great Plains states. The dust was so bad it choked livestock.

nation with food during the war years, farmers had plowed up too much sod. In the years after World War I, the rains stopped coming. By the 1930s, droughts had taken their toll. Without healthy crops or native grasses to hold down the sod, the dry soil simply blew away. Great swirls of black dust blanketed the plains.

The Dust Bowl era, as it came to be called, was part of a period known as the Great Depression. This was a time of severe economic hardship throughout the nation. Many people were out of work, and many families were going hungry. During the 1930s, the federal government created programs to help these families. Some federal money was used to create new housing.

The government also planted many trees in certain areas to block the winds that were blowing away so much valuable topsoil. Farmers learned more about protecting the soil, and eventually the land became useful again.

In 1941, the United States entered World War II (the war had started in Europe two years earlier). Going to war helped to end many of the country's economic troubles. While sixty-five thousand South Dakotans fought in the war, farmers and ranchers back home grew food to feed the nation and the world. The farmers of South Dakota pledged themselves to "raising food to win the war and dictate the peace." Families here often had their own victory gardens. Women knit olive-drab and navy scarves and sweaters for men serving their country.

Many South Dakotans worked in factories that produced supplies for the war effort. The state's factories made everything from tool kits to brass fittings used for military equipment. South Dakota's Homestake Mining Company switched its production during the war, converting its machine shops and **foundry** to make hand grenades and other hardware for the military.

Young South Dakotans were also important in supporting the war effort. Hundreds of young people, mostly from rural backgrounds, were trained in machine and radio repair, **aviation** mechanics, and welding, among other skills. Younger children collected scrap metal, such as tin cans, to be made into new goods needed by the armed forces.

On the Home Front

After World War II ended in 1945, South Dakota turned once again to its own needs. Cities slowly grew, creating new and different kinds of jobs. The federal government built four large dams on the Missouri River. The dams provided hydroelectric power (electricity created by using the power of flowing water), flood control, and irrigation for crops. First opened in 1941 as a training center for US bomber crews, Ellsworth Air Force Base, near Rapid City, expanded to become the state's most important military facility. Today, the base is home to about eight thousand people.

In the postwar period, the number of science and technology jobs increased. Technology spread to the world of farming. Today's farmers use computers and scientific instruments to do many tasks. These tasks include measuring seeds and water, destroying harmful insects, and saving crops from spoiling. With so much technology at work, far

Ellsworth Air Force Base continues to be an important military installation for the United States.

A Dinosaur Named Sue

In 1990, fossil hunter Sue Hendrickson was looking for dinosaur bones in South Dakota's Black Hills. Near the small community of Faith, she discovered the largest and most complete *T. rex* skeleton ever found. Today the skeleton, named Sue, is on display at the Field Museum in Chicago.

fewer people are needed to work on farms than in decades past. More people now live in South Dakota's cities and towns than in its rural areas. Changes in South Dakota's banking laws have made the state very attractive to credit-card companies. Other industries such as health services and telephone marketing have also become very important.

One of the state's leading centers of higher education is the University of South Dakota at Vermillion. Founded in 1862, it is South Dakota's oldest university. Nearly ten thousand students are enrolled at the school, which offers specialized programs in law, medicine, business, fine arts, and many other subjects. South Dakota is home to well over a dozen institutions of higher learning, including the Oglala Lakota College (OLC) located on the Pine Ridge Reservation. OLC offers degrees in a variety of subjects, ranging from business to Lakota studies.

Changes on the Reservations

Not all South Dakotans have benefited from the new industries. Prosperity has come slowly, if at all, to many of South Dakota's poorest residents, the Native Americans. Many Native American groups were forced onto reservations that had poor soils and that have not been well served by government programs. It has been hard for the members of South Dakota's tribes to replace their earlier way of life. Serious problems such as poverty, alcoholism, and unemployment are very common on the reservations.

In the 1960s, many Sioux decided that the time for change had come. An organization was formed called the American Indian Movement (AIM), led by Russell Means of the Pine Ridge Reservation. The movement's main goal was to show the rest of the country and the world the injustices endured by Native Americans. Means led a demonstration at the site where the Wounded Knee Massacre had taken place. He and his fellow Lakota Sioux protested conditions on the nation's reservations and wrongs that had been done to Native Americans. These included the breaking of treaties—especially the Fort Laramie Treaty of 1868, which had given the Black Hills to the Lakota "forever"—and the government's poor handling of Native American–owned funds and investments. For seventy-one days in 1973, AIM members occupied the small town of Wounded Knee

The Pine Ridge Reservation is home to thousands of Native Americans.

and held off federal agents until the government at last agreed to discuss the Fort Laramie Treaty.

On March 24, 1980, a case called *United States v. Sioux Nation of Indians* was argued before the US Supreme Court. In June, the court's nine justices ruled, eight to one, that the taking of the Black Hills was unfair and ordered the US government to pay for the land it had taken. The price for the Black Hills was set at $17.5 million, plus millions of dollars more in interest. Since the decision, the Sioux have refused the money, saying that they only want their land back.

By 2011, the amount of money set aside for a Black Hills settlement had grown to about $1.3 billion. Because there is still so much poverty on the reservations, some Native Americans have become more willing to accept the money. "It really saddens me that we've got some tribal members that want to accept the money," says Theresa Two Bulls, a former president of the Oglala Sioux (the Oglala are a subgroup of the Lakota Sioux). "They don't realize the harm they're going to do. They don't really understand why we say the Black Hills are sacred."

10 KEY DATES IN STATE HISTORY

1. 10,000-8000 BCE
Prehistoric humans known as Paleo-Indians live in the region, hunting mammoths and bison with stone weapons.

2. 500 CE
Mound Builders settle in villages along the Missouri River and the Big Sioux River. They are known for burying their dead under big mounds of dirt.

3. 1743
The Vérendrye brothers head south from Canada and lead a small exploration party in the region. They claim the area that is now South Dakota for France.

4. 1804
The Lewis and Clark expedition travels up the Missouri River through the Dakota region. They interact with several Native American groups, including the Yanktons, Arikaras, and Lakotas.

5. April 29, 1868
The Fort Laramie Treaty is signed, establishing the Great Sioux Reservation, which includes the Black Hills region. The treaty prohibits white settlement in the Black Hills.

6. November 2, 1889
South Dakota becomes the fortieth state. Its capital is established at Pierre.

7. December 29, 1890
Hundreds of Lakota men, women, and children are killed during the Wounded Knee Massacre on the Pine Ridge Reservation.

8. April 14, 1935
The date is remembered as Black Sunday because of a severe "black blizzard" caused by dry, dark soil blowing away in high winds.

9. February 27, 1973
American Indian Movement members occupy Wounded Knee. After a seventy-one-day standoff with federal agents, the US government agrees to discuss the Fort Laramie Treaty with the Sioux.

10. July 30, 2015
President Obama declares a dozen counties in South Dakota as federal disaster areas after they are hit by severe storms, tornadoes, flooding, and straight-line winds from June 17 to 24.

Native Americans comprise the largest minority group in South Dakota, and they contribute to its culture.

The People

Whether exploring South Dakota by foot, canoe, horseback, wagon, steamboat, train, automobile, motorcycle, or bicycle, travelers have always found plenty of places to stop and marvel. Millions have made their way across the state, and many hundreds of thousands have chosen to call it home.

Settling the Land

For more than a century, the Arikara tribe had South Dakota mostly to itself. In the mid-1700s, French trappers, traders, and missionaries passed through, sometimes pausing to set up a trading post or to introduce the Native Americans to Catholicism. At about the same time, the Sioux had begun their migration into the region. Before long, the area was the center of a rich culture belonging to a group once known as the Plains Indians. Deeply tied to the land, the Great Plains tribes rejoiced in its **bounty**. There was water, food, and shelter for all. As Lakota chief Red Cloud said, "The Great Spirit made us, the Indians, and gave us this land we live in. He gave us the buffalo, the antelope, and the deer for food and clothing … We were free as the winds."

Some French settlers eventually moved into the region, but most of them left once the trade in beaver pelts had ended. Farmers from the East soon arrived, however, leading

The mining town of Deadwood attracted people like Wild Bill Hickok and Calamity Jane.

their ox-driven wagons onto their new prairie farms. In the late 1800s, European immigrants joined in the Dakota homestead boom. When gold was discovered in the Black Hills, a new breed of adventure seekers also moved in.

The diversity of the people who settled this region can be seen in the colorful names of their counties and communities. Miners and other fortune hunters settled into towns they called Deadwood, Lead, and Shirttail Canyon.

Many places in South Dakota were named in honor of the European cities the immigrant pioneers left behind. Some examples are Bristol (England), Vienna (Austria), Stockholm (Sweden), and Tabor (in what is now the Czech Republic). Even South Dakota's state capital shows the European influence on the state. It bears a French name, Pierre (though it is pronounced "peer"). There are also places named after "back home" communities on the East Coast, such as Arlington (Virginia) and Amherst (Massachusetts). Throughout the state, Native American names are common, such as Oahe (a Sioux word meaning "something to stand on"), Oglala (a branch of the Lakota Sioux), or Minnehaha (a Sioux word meaning "falling water," or "waterfall").

A Wealth of Traditions

More than 85 percent of South Dakotans today are white, according to the last census. Most of them are of English, German, Irish, French, Russian, Portuguese, Scandinavian, or Czech ancestry. Many are related to the early homesteading families. More than seventy thousand Native Americans live in the state, making up almost 9 percent of the population. Many of these people live on one of the state's nine reservations: Cheyenne

There are many different recipes for kuchen.

River, Crow Creek, Flandreau, Lake Traverse, Lower Brule, Pine Ridge, Rosebud, Standing Rock, and Yankton. Hispanic Americans account for nearly 3 percent of the population. African-American and Asian-American residents each make up about 1 percent.

Each of the state's racial, ethnic, and cultural groups has added to South Dakota's fascinating and varied culture. Through the many diverse traditions, customs, foods, songs, stories, and festivals, South Dakota's rich heritage emerges. People of Czech descent celebrate Czech Days in Tabor with polka dances, ethnic costumes, and a delicious pastry called a *kolache*. When Swedish Americans near Sioux Falls gather for holidays, several appetizers are spread out in a style known as a smorgasbord. Norwegian Americans celebrate Norway's Independence Day on May 17 each year with parades, games, sports, and picnics.

People of German-Russian background hold a *Schmeckfest* in Eureka featuring sausage making, basket weaving, songfests, pioneer demonstrations, and healthy servings of a coffee cake called *kuchen*. This sweet dessert gets its name from the German word for "cake." Sometimes a kuchen looks like a pie; other times it appears like a typical coffee cake. There are as many recipes for kuchen as there are good cooks in South Dakota. Many recipes for kuchen call for a custard filling. You can also make kuchen with apples, cherries, berries, plums, peaches, cheese, or raisins. It's clear that South Dakotans love to eat kuchen—it was designated the state's official dessert in 2000.

Honoring South Dakota's Heritage

The Germans, French, and Irish brought the Catholic faith to the state, while Scandinavian settlers brought their Lutheran faith. Native Americans uphold their heritage at the many powwows held on their reservations. At powwows, some ceremonies are religious, such as the Sun Dance and the naming ceremony. In other events, men, women, and children take part in dance competitions, such as the grass dance, the fancy dance, or the jingle dress dance, as well as traditional activities such as storytelling and the gift-giving "giveaway."

★ 10 KEY PEOPLE ★ ★ ★

Tom Brokaw

Crazy Horse

Becky Hammon

1. Tom Brokaw

Born in 1940 on a farm in Webster, Tom Brokaw was the anchor of the NBC Nightly News for more than twenty years. Brokaw has also written *The Greatest Generation* and other best-selling books.

2. Vera Cleaver

Born in Virgil, Vera Cleaver started writing at age six. She and her husband, Bill Cleaver, wrote hundreds of articles, short stories, and novels. Some of their books, including *Sweetly Sings the Donkey* and *Dust of the Earth*, were set in South Dakota.

3. Shawn Colvin

Shawn Colvin is a singer-songwriter who taught herself to play guitar at age ten. She won the Grammy Award for Best Contemporary Folk Album in 1991 for *Steady On*. She's added vocals to songs by James Taylor and Sting, among others.

4. Crazy Horse

Crazy Horse, an Oglala Lakota chief, was born around 1840. In 1876, he led Sioux warriors to victory over the Seventh Cavalry in the Battle of the Little Bighorn. He was killed by soldiers while in prison on September 5, 1877.

5. Becky Hammon

Rapid City's Becky Hammon is a six-time all-star guard for the WNBA's New York Liberty and San Antonio Silver Stars. In 2014, she was hired as an assistant coach by the San Antonio Spurs, making her the first female coach in NBA history.

6. January Jones

January Jones was born in Brookings and went on to become a well-known TV and film actress. Her roles include Betty Draper in the TV series *Mad Men* and Emma Frost in the movie *X Men: First Class*.

7. Russell Means

Russell Means was a leading champion of Native American rights. As the first director of the American Indian Movement, he led demonstrations at Alcatraz Island, Plymouth Rock, and Wounded Knee. He also was an actor and an author.

8. Billy Mills

Billy Mills, whose Oglala Sioux name means "Loves His Country," was born on the Pine Ridge Reservation in 1938. A marine lieutenant, he won the 10,000-meter gold at the 1964 Tokyo Olympics, setting a world record. No other American has won that event in an Olympics.

9. Adam Vinatieri

Born in Yankton, Adam Vinatieri played football for South Dakota State University. As an NFL placekicker, he went on to win three Super Bowl titles with the New England Patriots and one with the Indianapolis Colts.

10. Laura Ingalls Wilder

Laura Ingalls Wilder (1867–1957) grew up in a pioneering farm family that eventually settled in what is now South Dakota. She wrote about the hardships and joys of life on the frontier in her many books, including *Little House on the Prairie*.

January Jones

Russell Means

Billy Mills

Who South Dakotans Are

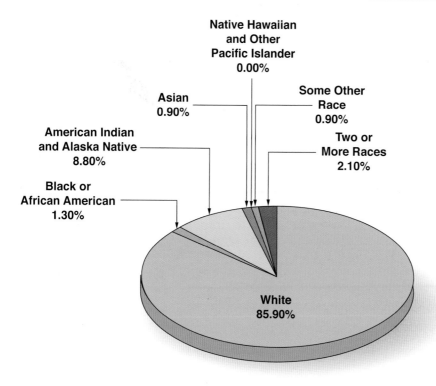

Native Hawaiian
and Other
Pacific Islander
0.00%

Asian
0.90%

American Indian
and Alaska Native
8.80%

Black or
African American
1.30%

Some Other
Race
0.90%

Two or
More Races
2.10%

White
85.90%

Total Population
814,180

Hispanic or Latino (of any race):
• Hispanic: 22,119 (2.7%)

Note: The pie chart shows the racial breakdown of the state's population based on the categories used by the US Bureau of the Census. The Census Bureau reports information for Hispanics or Latinos separately, since they may be of any race. Percentages in the pie chart may not add to 100 because of rounding.

Source: US Bureau of the Census, 2010 Census

Talking Turkey

Members of a small Protestant sect called the Hutterites live in fifty-four small rural colonies in South Dakota. The Hutterites don't believe in private ownership, choosing to share their property. Known for being excellent farmers, they produce more than 80 percent of the turkeys in South Dakota.

Traditional foods are also enjoyed, such as bison stew, tripe, fry bread, and *wojapi*, a type of pudding.

Although ethnic traditions run strong in South Dakota, other celebrations show off the state's unique charm. In Mitchell, a Russian-inspired building called the Corn Palace was erected to honor farmers and their harvest. Each year, during the harvest festival, fantastic murals made of corn and wheatgrass decorate the Corn Palace inside and out.

Rodeos, roundups, stampedes, and historical cavalry reenactments are some of the ways South Dakotans display their western frontier heritage. The colorful history of the Black Hills is played out each year in festivities such as Days of '76, the Badger Clark Cowboy Poetry and Music Gathering,

Children dress in traditional clothing for the powwow on the Pine Ridge Reservation.

Native Americans' Day at the Crazy Horse Memorial (South Dakota in 1990 became the first state to officially celebrate Native Americans' Day instead of Columbus Day), and the world-famous Sturgis Motorcycle Rally.

The Crazy Horse Volksmarch is an event held in the Black Hills that attracts thousands of visitors from around the world each year. A volksmarch is a large, organized hike. The story behind this celebration began in 1939, when Standing Bear, a Lakota official, asked the Polish-American sculptor Korczak Ziolkowski to carve a huge image of Crazy Horse into a mountain. He said, "My fellow chiefs and I would like the white man to know the [Native American] man has great heroes too." Standing Bear and Ziolkowski chose a site not far from Mount Rushmore in the Black Hills for the Crazy Horse Memorial. Ziolkowski believed in the project so much that he invested his own money. He began blasting at the site in 1948 but did not live to see his project completed. After his death, his family vowed to finish the monument. Twice a year, visitors are offered an up-close view of the work in progress. During the volksmarch, they climb the 741 steps up to the almost 600-foot (183 m) carving of Crazy Horse.

Small Towns, Open Spaces

"The whole of South Dakota is one big small town," says a rancher from Echo Valley. Population numbers are proof of that. According to the 2010 US census, the United States averaged 87.4 people per 1 square mile (2.5 sq km). This was much higher than South Dakota's average of just 10.7 people per square mile.

Only the state's largest city, Sioux Falls, has more than 150,000 people. Rapid City is the state's second-largest city, with close to 68,000 people. After that, the populations of other cities are much smaller. Vermillion, with a population of about 10,600, is home to the University of South Dakota. People in town were very surprised and excited when an article about the good life in Vermillion appeared in a major national newspaper, the *Wall Street Journal*. Community leaders boasted about the article in a local newspaper: "In Vermillion the cost of living is affordable, there is low crime, good education, good climate, a good work force …"

The 2010 census reported that South Dakota ranked forty-sixth among the fifty states in number of residents. The state also placed forty-sixth among the states in population density. Only four states—North Dakota, Montana, Wyoming, and Alaska—had lower population densities.

Residents in other parts of the state report that living in a small city or town in South Dakota gives you choices. There are many theaters, parks, galleries, and museums to visit, such as the Museum of Geology in Rapid City, the Dakota Discover Museum in Mitchell, the Black Hills Mining Museum in Lead, or the South Dakota Air and Space Museum near Ellsworth Air Force Base. South Dakotans can also head for the "wide open spaces" and enjoy nature and the outdoors.

Friends and Neighbors

While South Dakota communities are close knit, they do have their share of problems. Farming and ranching are difficult ways to make a living. Many young people no longer want to live on a remote farm, and a number of small towns are losing younger residents to bigger cities. "Most of our towns are really just retirement towns," says one lifelong resident.

The same problem also exists on South Dakota's Native American reservations. When Native American students leave for college, they seldom return. People shake their heads sadly when they think about the new ideas and technical skills the young people could bring to their communities, if only they came back home after college graduation. "It's hard these days," says one resident. "You don't want to get stale. You have to be creative to make it all work, or you will lose it."

Poverty, sickness, and a lack of opportunities also make life on the reservation a challenge for some. Unemployment on the reservations, such as Rosebud and Pine Ridge, sometimes reaches over 80 percent. It's very common for the heads of Native American families to leave the reservation in search of work. Extended families often pool their resources in an effort to provide for their basic needs. Many Native Americans live in overcrowded housing conditions because families try not to turn away even extended

The courageous SuAnne Big Crow left a proud legacy that is still helping people years after her untimely death.

family members in need of a place to stay. Homelessness is also a serious problem on the reservations.

A young Oglala woman named SuAnne Big Crow was very creative in her short life. SuAnne played basketball on the Pine Ridge high school team, nicknamed the Lady Thorpes. She was loved not only for her athletic skills, but also for her kindness. After graduating, she planned to go to college and then return to Pine Ridge, in order to help her people.

One night, she became a hero to many more than the people of Pine Ridge. The Lady Thorpes were preparing to play the Lead high school team. Before the game, the people in the gym began to call out war whoops and other taunts that mocked the Native American team. The Lady Thorpes' captain was afraid to leave the locker room and face the jeering crowd, so SuAnne said she would go. She stood in the center of the gymnasium and bowed her head. Then, she removed her warm-up jacket and used it to perform a traditional shawl dance. The crowd grew quiet, and before long, the spectators understood SuAnne's proud act of courage. Soon, everyone began to cheer. The Lady Thorpes won the game, and the team went on to tour Europe.

Tragically, SuAnne was killed in an automobile accident, but her vision for Pine Ridge lives on. Her dream of a "rainbow place" where children on the reservation can play safely is now a reality. The SuAnne Big Crow Boys and Girls Club of Pine Ridge is an exciting example of South Dakotans of all ages working together to build stronger communities.

1. Corn Palace Harvest Festival

In late August, South Dakotans decorate the Corn Palace in Mitchell with murals made of corn and wheat. They celebrate their harvest with food, carnival rides, and a rodeo. Live entertainment attracts people from all over the state.

2. Czech Days Celebration in Tabor

Every June, thousands of people come to Tabor to celebrate Czech heritage. They enjoy parades, polka music, traditional costumes, dances, baking demonstrations, and the tasty Czech pastry kolache. There's even a race called the Kolache Krawl.

3. Frontier Christmas at Fort Sisseton

Visitors step back in time to celebrate an old-fashioned Christmas at one of the best-preserved forts of the American frontier. Activities include storytelling, music, and sleigh rides. There are also make-and-take craft sessions, festive treats, and a visit from Father Christmas.

4. German-Russian Schmeckfest

This September celebration in Eureka honors the German-Russian immigrants who left Russia for the prairies of South Dakota. Schmeckfest activities include music, dance, pioneer demonstrations, a golf tournament, and traditional foods such as kuchen.

5. Laura Ingalls Wilder Pageant

In July, tourists visit De Smet for a taste of the pioneer experience. Spectators sit on blankets and lawn chairs to watch actors re-create scenes from the author's *Little House* books, near the site of the Ingalls family's South Dakota homestead.

Corn Palace Harvest Festival

Czech Days Celebration in Tabor

SOUTH DAKOTA

6. Potato Day Celebration

Since farmers here grow bushels of spuds, the town of Clark hosts a Potato Day celebration each year. Besides a cooking contest for potato dishes, awards are given for the Best Decorated Potato. Brave adults can wrestle in mashed potatoes!

7. Rhubarb Festival

The town of Leola (which calls itself the Rhubarb Capital of the World) hosts this fun summer festival. Rhubarb royalty are crowned, rhubarb desserts are judged, turtles are raced, and awards are presented for the tallest rhubarb structure.

8. Sisseton-Wahpeton Wacipi

This powwow is the oldest event of its kind in South Dakota. For more than a century, Sioux people have gathered in Agency Village to sing, dance, pray, honor friendships, and feast together. The event is held in early July.

9. South Dakota State Fair

More than two hundred thousand people attend the state fair in Huron, held in late August and early September. The event is loaded with agricultural and craft exhibits, livestock shows, rodeos, car races, farm machinery displays, carnival rides, and more.

10. Sturgis Motorcycle Rally

Each August, hundreds of thousands of motorcycle riders gather in the small mountain town of Sturgis, in western South Dakota. Participants can enjoy concerts, races, and lively celebrations. Vendors show off a wide variety of bikes.

South Dakota State Fair

Sturgis Motorcycle Rally

Pierre has been the capital of South Dakota since it became a state.

How the Government Works

S outh Dakota has many levels of government, including municipal, county, state, federal, and tribal. The state is divided into sixty-six counties. South Dakota voters elect commissioners to run county governments. Mayors or councils are elected to run the state's three hundred-plus municipal governments in cities, towns, or villages. Each reservation has a tribal government. Leaders are elected to tribal councils.

Pierre has been the capital since South Dakota became a state in 1889. Voters elect the state's top executive officers and members of the state legislature. Elected executive officials include the governor, lieutenant governor, secretary of state, attorney general, state auditor, state treasurer, and various commissioners. The state legislature has two houses, or chambers: the senate and the house of representatives.

For representation in the federal government, South Dakotans elect two US senators and one member of the US House of Representatives.

Branches of Government

Executive

The governor is the executive branch's chief officer. He or she is the head of the state. The governor may serve only two four-year terms in a row. The governor's duties include

Governor Dennis Daugaard delivers his State of the State speech in 2012 in the legislative chambers.

preparing the state budget, suggesting new laws, and selecting important officials. He or she must also sign bills into law or reject them, which is called a **veto**. Each year the governor gives a speech to the legislature called the State of the State address. It addresses issues facing the state and actions the governor thinks the government should take to deal with those issues.

Silly Law

It is illegal to lie down and fall sleep in a cheese factory in South Dakota.

Legislative

The legislative branch, or state legislature, consists of a thirty-five-member senate and a seventy-member house of representatives. Voters in each of the state's thirty-five legislative districts can vote for one senator and two representatives. All members of the legislature are elected for two-year terms. They cannot hold the same seat for more than four terms in a row. Legislators meet each year in the state capital, Pierre. When not in session, they have other occupations. Some are farmers, teachers, lawyers, or homemakers.

Judicial

The judicial branch is a system of state courts. The state's highest court is the South Dakota Supreme Court. It consists of a chief justice and four associate justices who are first appointed by the governor for a three-year period and later elected by voters for eight-year terms. The justices oversee other courts, decide **appeals** of lower-court decisions, and advise the executive branch on legal matters. Circuit courts are the general trial courts that make decisions on serious crimes and lawsuits. The lower courts (called magistrate courts) rule on small claims and lesser crimes like traffic violations.

Initiative and Referendum

In 1898, South Dakota citizens were the first in the country to decide on a method of lawmaking called initiative and referendum. In an initiative, people sign a petition asking for a certain law to be created. For an initiative to gain a place on the ballot, the

Petitions are piled up as citizens attempt to collect enough signatures to force a referendum in 2006.

petition must be signed by at least five percent of the total number of people who voted for governor in the last election. If enough people vote for the initiative on Election Day, it becomes a law without having to be passed by the legislature or signed by the governor. In a referendum, people sign a petition asking that an existing law be changed or removed. If enough people vote for the referendum, then the existing law is changed or struck down.

Not all states allow this process. Some that do allow it have had serious problems, such as creating laws that harm the state economy. But South Dakotans have tended to choose their petitions wisely. As a senator told voters, "I've seen firsthand how well this can work. South Dakotans have taken this responsibility very seriously, using it sparingly and sensibly."

How a Bill Becomes a Law

Although laws can be adopted by initiative, most laws in South Dakota are created by the legislature. Some bills (proposed laws) begin in the state house of representatives. Others begin in the state senate. In either case, the procedures followed to consider the bill are similar. To begin, a legislator with an idea for a law drafts the bill. Later, he or she presents the bill to the bill clerk. After the clerk gives the bill a number, the process is under way.

After the chief clerk reads the bill aloud, the bill is assigned to a committee. There are many committees. Each focuses on a subject, such as agriculture, education, natural resources, health, commerce, transportation, or taxes. Copies of the bill are printed and given to committee members and other interested citizens. Committee meetings are open to the public. During the meetings, members review the bill. They listen to people who come to talk about why they favor or oppose the bill. If the committee approves the bill, the next day it is read aloud a second time to the entire house.

At this point, house members can debate and suggest changes to the bill. Once the exact wording of the bill is decided, a vote is taken. If a majority votes in favor, then the bill moves on to the other chamber of the legislature, where the process of considering the bill is repeated. If the second chamber makes changes to the bill before passing it, a conference committee may be chosen to work out the differences between the two versions. Then, both chambers must pass the revised bill before it can be delivered to the governor. If the governor signs the bill, it becomes law. If the governor rejects, or vetoes, the bill, it's returned to the legislature. The members of the legislature must then decide whether to overturn the governor's veto. Two-thirds of both houses must vote in favor of the bill to reverse the veto and allow the bill to become law.

Everyone Has a Voice

South Dakotans strongly believe that every person's voice counts. Preserving the family farm has long been an important issue for state voters. Ninety percent of South Dakota's land is devoted to agriculture. The state has more than thirty-one thousand farms. Family farmers and ranchers say the profits from large-scale corporate farms end up in corporate headquarters, not in the local economy. The idea of South Dakotan farmers working their own land to benefit a distant corporation sends many voters to the polls. As rancher Ron Ogren commented, "It's important to … help ourselves."

In 1974, the state legislature passed the Family Farm Act, which recognized the importance of family farms and the threat posed to them by corporate farming. In the November 1998 election, the majority of South Dakotan voters passed a referendum called Amendment E. This referendum banned large corporations from operating certain kinds of farms in South Dakota. Amendment E became a part of the state constitution. In 2003, a federal court ruled that this ban violated the US Constitution. Even though Amendment E was overturned, South Dakota voters have continued to fight for family farmers' rights.

An act limiting ownership of farms, passed by a referendum, was ruled unconstitutional.

In Their Own Words

"One thing that stands out throughout the entire year was that in South Dakota we are much more united than we are divided. Now the divided part creates news, but the united part is what moves us forward."
—South Dakota governor Mike Rounds

In 1992, some schools chose to start a Kids Voting Day. This program, now called Kids Voting South Dakota, involves about eighty thousand young people. Students from kindergarten through high school study the way government works. They read about and debate the political issues of the day. On Election Day, they go with their parents to real polling places and cast their votes. The results of the students' votes, which do not really help decide the election and are counted separately, are reported by the state's news media.

Lawmakers believe the program helps everyone. Students learn about the importance of taking part in the election process. And after getting involved at school, many students talk about the issues with their families and encourage their parents to vote.

Tom Daschle: US Congressman, 1979-1985; US Senator, 1987-2005

Born in Aberdeen, Tom Daschle served in the US Air Force as an intelligence officer. A major influence in the Democratic Party, he was the senate majority leader of the 107th Congress before losing a re-election bid in 2004. Daschle served as an adviser to President Barack Obama before becoming a registered lobbyist for Taiwan.

Hubert Humphrey: Vice President, 1965-1969

In 1911, Hubert Humphrey was born in Wallace. He was elected mayor of Minneapolis in 1945. Humphrey served as a US senator from 1948 to 1964, and 1971 to 1978, championing causes like civil rights. After serving as vice president under Lyndon Johnson, Humphrey lost the 1968 presidential election and returned to the Senate.

George McGovern: US Congressman, 1957-1961; US Senator, 1963-1981

After serving as a bomber pilot in World War II, George McGovern was director of the Food for Peace Program under President John F. Kennedy. He then won election to the US Senate. He also won the 1972 Democratic Party's presidential nomination, but he lost in the general election to President Richard Nixon.

SOUTH DAKOTA
YOU CAN MAKE A DIFFERENCE

Contacting Lawmakers

If there is something you feel strongly about in your community or your state, you can try contacting one of South Dakota's governmental officials. Here's how to do it:

To contact the governor, go to the following website:

sd.gov/Governor/contactheader.aspx.

Here you will see a link where you can email South Dakota's governor directly. All you have to do is fill in your name, address, and your question or comment.

To contact South Dakota's state legislators, go to this website:

legis.sd.gov/Legislators/Legislators/default.aspx?CurrentSession=True.

On the left-hand side of the screen, you could click on the link where it says "Find Legislator for Address." Type in your address, and the names, photos, and contact details of your three representatives would appear on the screen. You could then email your representative.

To contact your national representatives, go to the following website:

www.govtrack.us/congress/members/SD.

A New Holiday in South Dakota

Cattle ranching has been an important part of South Dakota history since its earliest days. The men and women who work on dairy farms and cattle ranches have done much for the economy of the state. Their hard work ethic represents the tough pioneer spirit that's been a part of the South Dakota way of life for generations.

Some South Dakota citizens wanted to see the proud cowboy heritage celebrated in the form of an official holiday. During the 2014 legislative session, a bill (number 1184) was proposed to see the fourth Saturday of July dedicated as a holiday called the Day of the American Cowboy.

Bill 1184 was first read aloud in the South Dakota House of Representatives on January 30, 2014. It was passed **unanimously** in both the South Dakota Senate and House of Representatives. Finally, on March 14, Governor Dennis Daugaard signed the bill into law. The Day of the American Cowboy was created for celebrating the "protection, preservation, and promotion of the cowboy and Western heritage of the State of South Dakota, and honoring the cowboys and cowgirls for their enduring contribution to the courageous, pioneering spirit of America."

Hay and sunflowers are two of the most valuable crops grown in South Dakota.

Making a Living

The Missouri River does more than split South Dakota through the middle. It divides the way citizens make a living. As author John Steinbeck wrote in *Travels with Charley*, "The two sides of the river might well be a thousand miles apart." East River, as the land east of the Missouri River is called, is rolling farmland dotted with small cities and towns. Communities are more closely spaced, farms are smaller, and the population is greater. West River, on the other hand, is dry and rugged. People and towns are farther apart in this land of cattle ranches, windmills, mountains, and the Badlands.

Farming

No matter which side of the divide South Dakotans live on, they live close to the land. As one East River farmer boasted, "My great-grandfather farmed when grasses were as tall as a horse's ear." Farmers now raise rows of sunflowers, flax, hay, wheat, rye, and corn, as well as dairy cattle and poultry. About one of every fourteen workers in South Dakota works in agriculture.

Farmers are proud of their heritage and their families' ties to the land. However, it's becoming more and more of a struggle to afford to operate a farm. Farmers say it takes about 3,000 to 4,000 acres (about 1,200 to 1,600 ha) to support one family. Crops need rain. South Dakota's unreliable rainfall, plus the high cost of supplies, taxes, and land, means that many farmers struggle to pay the bills. Modern equipment is another added expense. Many farmers now have a computer in the tractor cab for downloading satellite photos that track crops growing in the fields and the movements of livestock. Said one farming couple, "It's not for the faint of heart, this lifestyle, but it's worth all the challenges and high blood pressure."

Wonderful Winds

Windy conditions are common on the prairies of South Dakota. While some folks may find the winds tough to take at times, they can also be good. The National Renewable Energy Laboratory estimates that 88 percent of the land in South Dakota is suitable for wind power.

City Life

Sioux Falls and other cities east of the Missouri River, such as Brookings, Yankton, Mitchell, and Vermillion, offer many different ways to make a living. The unemployment rate in South Dakota's cities is very low. This is sometimes credited to the state's low taxes and good business climate. These cities offer jobs in manufacturing food products, farm equipment, tools, and machinery. People can also find jobs in high-technology fields such as computers

Meatpacking plants and other food processing facilities give jobs to many people in South Dakota.

and telecommunications. For example, a company called Daktronics (the name is a combination of the words "Dakota" and "electronics") is located in Brookings. This company employs many workers and is one of the country's largest makers of sports video displays. Almost every NFL stadium has some equipment made by Daktronics.

Also in Brookings is Falcon Plastics, which has increased greatly in size since its founding in 1975 and now employs people with more technical skills due to automation.

The banking and credit-card industry is very important in the state, and many South Dakotans also find employment in service industries such as health care, retail sales, entertainment, and publishing. Pierre, the capital, is located in the center of the state. Many workers there hold jobs in government and other service fields.

Western Resources

West of the Missouri River, ranchers raise herds of beef cattle and bison on dry scrub grass rangelands. While cattle ranching is big business on the Great Plains, raising bison is a small but growing trend. Bison meat (usually sold as buffalo steaks, stew meat, or burgers) is rich in protein and low in fat. Many people believe that the amazing strength of the people of the Plains tribes was due in large part to a diet of this meat. Today, there are herds grazing on public lands such as Custer State Park and Wind Cave National Park, and on all of South Dakota's tribal lands.

Along with raising bison and other agricultural products, residents of South Dakota's tribal reservations are finding new ways to earn a living. Many work in tribal-run gaming **casinos**, which provide an important source of income for the tribes. On the Rosebud Sioux Reservation, tribal members have built a high-tech wind farm. The wind farm, which came online in May 2003, produces more than enough energy to power a large casino complex throughout the year. Some of the excess power is sold to Ellsworth Air Force Base.

In the Badlands and the Black Hills, workers take on many different types of jobs. They are park rangers, forest workers, loggers, mill workers, miners, cowboys, tour guides, and **geologists**, just to name a few occupations. Although about 4 percent of South Dakota is forested, loggers have been cutting large quantities of ponderosa pine and white spruce in the Black Hills since 1899. Also, as soon as George Armstrong Custer reported, "Gold has been found," the cities of Deadwood and Lead became home to mine workers. However, the Homestake Mine in Lead, which was one of the nation's largest gold mines for more than a century, shut down completely in 2003. Extending 4,850 feet (1,480 m) underground, the mine had already been used for science experiments. Plans call for the

★10 KEY★ INDUSTRIES

1. Bees and Honey

South Dakota ranks among the nation's leaders in honey production. Annual honey output in the state has reached more than 21 million pounds (9.5 million kilograms) of honey from about 225,000 hives.

2. Credit Cards

Several large credit-card companies are located in South Dakota. These include Citibank, Wells Fargo, and Target and Sears (credit cards). About twenty thousand people in Sioux Falls work in the financial services industry. Jobs include processing new credit cards and providing customer service.

3. Government

The government employs thousands of workers in South Dakota at the federal, state, local or county levels. Government workers hold all kinds of jobs from city mayors to national park rangers to managing grazing rights on federal lands.

4. Granite

Granite outcroppings in South Dakota were formed during the last Ice Age. Today, the state is one of the leading producers of granite. Mahogany granite is a deep red stone quarried in South Dakota. It's used in floor tiles, countertops, and monuments.

5. Livestock

Raising livestock is a huge industry in South Dakota. Farmers and ranchers raise cattle, pigs, turkeys, and sheep, among other animals. The state is also the nation's top producer of bison, producing over 20 percent of the total in the United States.

Bees and Honey

Credit Cards

6. Manufacturing

Many products are made throughout the state. These products include medical equipment, computers, computer parts, and the electronic scoreboards seen in sports stadiums. Meat, grains, and cheese are examples of foods processed in South Dakota.

7. Mining

South Dakota is mineral-rich, with a number of mining operations working around the state. Just west of the old mining town of Lead is the operational Wharf gold mine. Construction sand and gravel are still mined in South Dakota.

8. Seeds and Grains

Plenty of sun and water help make South Dakota the second-largest producer of sunflower seeds in the nation. About 86 percent of these sunflower seeds are used for birdseed or for sunflower oil. The state is also a major producer of wheat, corn, and soybeans.

9. Tourism

Visitors coming from around the world to South Dakota mean big business to the state. Tourists bring in about $2 billion each year. Attractions include Mount Rushmore, the Badlands, the Crazy Horse Memorial, and the Black Hills.

10. Waterpower

The Oahe Dam is one of the United States' largest dams. At 245 feet (75 m) high, it produces electricity for South Dakota and four neighboring states. In 2013, the state produced nearly 40 percent of its electricity from hydropower.

Livestock

Waterpower

Recipe for Sunflower Seed Cookies

South Dakota is the second-biggest sunflower seed producer in the United States. Sunflower seeds are tasty and add a nutty flavor to baked goods. They're also full of good nutrition.

What You Need

1 stick (4 ounces, or 120 milliliters)
   butter, softened

½ cup (120 mL) sugar

1 cup (240 mL) flour

1¼ cups (300 mL) rolled oats, either
   regular or quick-cooking

½ teaspoon (2.5 mL) salt

1½ teaspoons (7.5 mL) vanilla

¾ teaspoons (4 mL) baking powder

½ cup (120 mL) grated coconut

½ cup (120 mL) sunflower seeds

1 egg

What To Do

- Preheat the oven to 350°F (175°C). Ask an adult to help you with the oven. Line two cookie sheets with parchment paper and set aside.

- While the oven is heating, mix the butter and sugar until fluffy, using an electric mixer. Add the egg, salt, and vanilla and beat until just combined. Stir in the sunflower seeds and the coconut.

- In a different bowl, mix oats, baking powder, and flour. Then add this dry mix to the butter mixture. Stir until everything is completely combined.

- Use a tablespoon or cookie scoop to drop rounded tablespoons of dough onto the parchment-lined cookie sheets. Bake for 10 to 12 minutes, until lightly browned. Set aside to cool.

The Large Underground Xenon Detector, used for particle research, was built inside the former Homestake Mine.

abandoned mine to be permanently transformed into a laboratory that will detect earthquakes and help unlock some of the mysteries of **physics**.

Because there are fewer people in western South Dakota, there are fewer cities. Rapid City is the largest and is a regional center for much of the Great Plains. The South Dakota School of Mines and Technology in Rapid City is a hub for engineering and the study of geology. Scientists, rock hounds, and archaeologists have long been drawn to the area's incredible fossils and rock samples. Several important fossils have been discovered in the region.

Tourism in the West

Tourism is a fast-growing industry in South Dakota. Most tourists head for the western portion of the state, seeking historic sites, outdoor recreation, wildlife, and spectacular scenery at such destinations as the Black Hills, Badlands National Park, Custer State Park, Wind Cave National Park, Mount Rushmore, and the Crazy Horse Memorial. Mount Rushmore has long been a very popular destination, receiving nearly three million visitors a year. Travelers on the road to Mount Rushmore will see countless signs promising "Free Ice Water" at Wall Drug. Once a tiny store in a town forgotten during the Great Depression of the 1930s, Wall Drug Store prospered after its owners posted road signs advertising free ice water. Soon tourists came in droves, drank the ice water, and bought souvenirs. Wall Drug now takes up most of the town and features restaurants, dozens of shops, and of course, free ice water.

The former Black Hills mining town of Deadwood has also looked to tourism to keep its economy healthy. With nearly all of the mines shut down, the community remade itself into a "Wild West" town featuring gambling casinos and reenactments of the lives of famous gold-rush characters such as Wild Bill Hickok and Calamity Jane. Another town, Spearfish, attracts hunters, hikers, river rafters, and fishers from all over the country, while each year

The Sturgis Motorcycle Rally attracts hundreds of thousands of people to South Dakota.

the nearby town of Sturgis hosts hundreds of thousands of motorcycle riders in the Sturgis Motorcycle Rally.

Restoring the Big Muddy

The Missouri River has always been important to the state's history. In 1804, Lewis and Clark marveled at the Big Muddy. They also described and illustrated many plants and animals found along its banks. A hundred years later, writer George Fitch called the river "tawny, restless, brawling."

Once pioneers settled along the river, they put it to work for them. The river watered their crops, powered their mill wheels, and transported their supplies. The river also flooded their fields and homes, washed away riverbanks, and formed sandbars that damaged and wrecked boats. By the 1960s, dams had been built. They prevented floods, slowed soil erosion, made electricity from waterpower, and created navigation channels for barges. They also formed four large reservoirs known as the Great Lakes of South Dakota. These lakes provide recreational activities such as boating, swimming, and fishing. Today, however, many say that the Missouri River is one of the country's most endangered

People in South Dakota are working to restore the Missouri River to its natural state.

Lots of Honey/Bee-ing Productive

On average, a worker bee will produce up to 1 teaspoon (5 mL) of honey in her lifetime (about forty-five days). An average hive will make about 2 pounds (0.9 kg) of honey in a day. South Dakota's beekeepers produced 14.8 million pounds (6.7 million kg) of honey in 2014 alone.

rivers. The dams have changed the path of the Big Muddy, reducing the breeding grounds for fish and other species. Pollution from industries along the waterway has also harmed the river. Author Stephen Ambrose said, "The river has been damaged … It's a great big ditch."

Citizens are hoping to change that. They say that there are other ways to run the dams that will help the economy and restore the river to its former "tawny, restless, brawling" self. By making the river cleaner and healthier for fish and wildlife, the state will earn more money from increased tourism. With the help of new technology, fresh ideas, and a willingness to work hard, South Dakotans have much to look forward to. As South Dakota pioneer and novelist Ole Rolvaag described in his book *Giants in the Earth*, South Dakotans can see a "bright, clear sky, today, tomorrow, and for all time to come."

SOUTH DAKOTA
STATE MAP

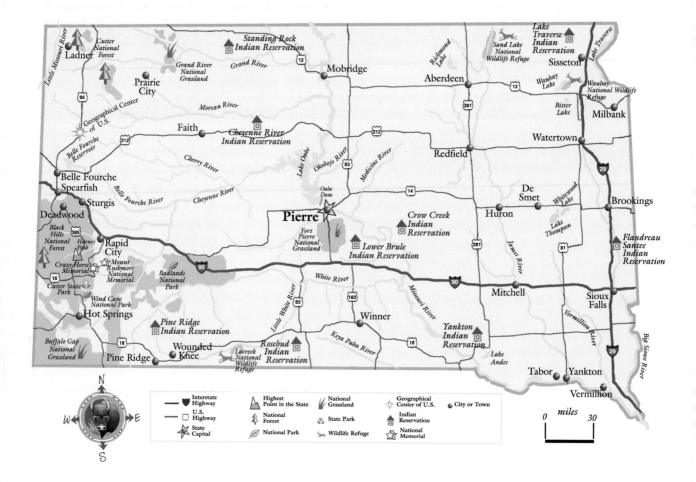

Little Missouri River
Ladner
Custer National Forest
Grand River National Grassland
Standing Rock Indian Reservation
Grand River
12
Mobridge
Richmond Lake
Sand Lake National Wildlife Refuge
Lake Traverse Indian Reservation
Lake Traverse
Sisseton
Prairie City
85
Geographical Center of U.S.
Moreau River
Aberdeen
281
12
Waubay Lake
Waubay National Wildlife Refuge
Belle Fourche Reservoir
Faith
Cheyenne River Indian Reservation
212
Cherry River
Lake Oahe
Okobojo River
212
Medicine River
Redfield
83
Bitter Lake
Milbank
Watertown
Belle Fourche
Spearfish
Belle Fourche River
Cheyenne River
Oahe Dam
Pierre
14
Huron
De Smet
Whitewood Lake
29
Brookings
Sturgis
Deadwood
Black Hills National Forest
Harney Peak
385
Rapid City
Crazy Horse Memorial
Mount Rushmore National Memorial
16
Custer State Park
Wind Cave National Park
Hot Springs
Badlands National Park
90
Fort Pierre National Grassland
Lower Brule Indian Reservation
Crow Creek Indian Reservation
281
James River
Lake Thompson
81
Flandreau Santee Indian Reservation
White River
90
Mitchell
Sioux Falls
Vermillion River
Buffalo Gap National Grassland
18
Pine Ridge
Wounded Knee
Lacreek National Wildlife Refuge
Pine Ridge Indian Reservation
Little White River
83
Rosebud Indian Reservation
Keya Paha River
183
Winner
Missouri River
18
Yankton Indian Reservation
Lake Andes
Tabor
Yankton
29
Big Sioux River
Vermillion

Legend
Interstate Highway
U.S. Highway
State Capital
Highest Point in the State
National Forest
National Park
National Grassland
State Park
Wildlife Refuge
Geographical Center of U.S.
Indian Reservation
National Memorial
City or Town

N
W E
S

miles
0   30

SOUTH DAKOTA
MAP SKILLS

1. In which direction would you travel to get from Watertown to Hot Springs?

2. The city of Deadwood lies within which national forest?

3. About how many miles is it from Mobridge to Aberdeen?

4. Which highway connects the cities of Spearfish and Sioux Falls?

5. What city lies closest to the Grand River National Grassland?

6. Which river connects the cities of Huron and Mitchell?

7. What national wildlife refuge is closest to Wounded Knee?

8. In which direction would you travel to get from Faith to the Cheyenne River Indian Reservation?

9. What large lake lies north of South Dakota's state capital?

10. Which national park lies between Rapid City and Mitchell along Interstate 90?

Lake Oahe

Lacreek National Wildlife Refuge

10. Badlands National Park
9. Lake Oahe
8. East
7. Lacreek National Wildlife Refuge
6. James River
5. Prairie City
4. Interstate 90
3. About 100 miles (161 km)
2. Black Hills National Forest
1. Southwest

State Flag, Seal, and Song

The state flag of South Dakota is sky blue with the great seal of South Dakota in the center. "South Dakota, the Mount Rushmore State" is printed around the seal.

On a blue background, the state seal features golden circles surrounding a farmer plowing with a team of horses. There is a field with cattle and a steamboat going upriver past a smoking mill, with hills in the distance. The words in the seal declare, "Under God the People Rule." The year of statehood, 1889, is included.

The state of South Dakota chose its official state song by contest. Nearly eighty songs were submitted for consideration. The winning song, titled "Hail! South Dakota," was composed and written by DeeCort Hammitt. Hammitt was a teacher and band director in Alcester, a small town in southeastern South Dakota. This song celebrates the state's spectacular scenery, from the Black Hills to the farms and prairies to the Mount Rushmore National Monument. "Hail! South Dakota" was adopted as the state's official song on March 5, 1943.

To view the song's lyrics, visit: **www.50states.com/songs/sdakota.htm#.VjOsaqKAL-s**.

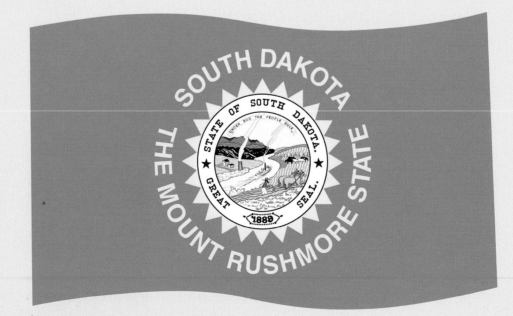

Glossary

appeal   A legal proceeding by which a case is brought to a higher court for review.

archaeologist   A person who studies past human life as shown by the monuments, tools, and fossil relics left behind by ancient people.

aviation   The flying or operating of aircraft

bounty   An abundance of something; plenty.

casino   A building or room used for gambling.

debris   An accumulation of rock fragments or the remains of something that has broken down.

epidemic   A widespread outbreak of an infectious disease in a community.

erosion   The processing of wearing away rock or soil by the action of water, wind, or glacial ice.

foundry   A factory or building where metals are cast. Metals are cast into shapes by pouring melted metal into molds.

geologist   A person who studies the history of the Earth, particularly as recorded in rocks.

indigenous   Originating (as a group of people) in a particular place; native.

massacre   The violent killing of many often defenseless people.

paleontological   Dealing with the study of life of past geological periods, especially as known from fossil remains.

physics   The science dealing with matter and energy and their actions upon each other.

refuge   A place that provides protection or shelter (often for wildlife).

spire   A sharp pointed tip, such as a rock formation or a top of a building.

unanimously   Having been agreed to by all, as in a voting process.

veto   The power of the head of a government to prevent a bill passed by a legislature from becoming a law.

More About South Dakota

BOOKS

Burgan, Michael. *South Dakota*. New York: Children's Press, 2014.

Meinking, Mary. *What's Great About South Dakota?* Our Great States. Minneapolis, MN: Lerner Publishing Group, Inc., 2015.

Nelson, S.D. *Sitting Bull: Lakota Warrior And Defender Of His People*. New York: Harry N. Abrams, 2015.

Woog, Adam. *Calamity Jane*. Legends of the Wild West. New York: Chelsea House, 2010.

WEBSITES

Mount Rushmore National Memorial

www.nps.gov/moru/index.htm

South Dakota Department of Tourism Website

www.travelsd.com

South Dakota State Government Website

sd.gov

ABOUT THE AUTHORS

Ruth Bjorklund lives on Bainbridge Island, a ferry ride from Seattle, and has contributed to many titles in the It's My State! series.

Geoffrey M. Horn was an experience writer/editor who worked at the Macmillan publishing house before becoming a freelancer. He passed away in 2013 in Red Bank, New Jersey.

Alicia Klepeis began her career at the National Geographic Society. She is the author of numerous children's books.

Index

Page numbers in **boldface** are illustrations. Entries in **boldface** are glossary terms.

American Indian Movement, 41–43, 49
appeal, 58
archaeologist, 24, 71
Arikara (tribe), 24–26, 28, 43, 45
aviation, 39

Badlands, 9, 12–14, **13**, 16–17, 65, 67, 69, 71
Big Crow, SuAnne, 53, **53**
birds, 4, 8–9, 16–18, 20–21
bison, 7, 9, 13–14, 16–17, **18**, 20, 23, **24**, 25–28, 31, 43, 50, 67–68
Black Hills, 4, **6**, 13–14, 16–17, 31–32, 37, 41–43, 46, 50–52, 67, 69, 71
Borglum, Gutzon, 15, 37
bounty, 45
Brookings, 8, 34, 49, 66–67

casino, 67, 71
cattle, 63, 65, 67–68

caves, 7, 15–17, 67, 71
climate, 7, 18–19, 68
Corn Palace, 14, 35, 50, 54
coyotes, 5, 7, 9, **9**, 16
Crazy Horse, 14, 31, 48, 51
Crazy Horse Memorial, 14, 51, 69, 71

Dakota (tribe), 25–26
dams, 9, **12**, 39, 69, 72–73
Deadwood, 32, 46, **46**, 67, 71
debris, 8, 12

Ellsworth Air Force Base, 39, **40**, 52, 67
epidemic, 28
erosion, 14, 72

farming, 8–9, 12, 16–18, 24–25, 31, 33, 36–40, **38**, 45–46, 50, 52, 55, 58, 60, **64**, 65–66
Fort Laramie Treat, 31, 41–43
fossils, 5, 7, **8**, 12, 14–16, **17**, **22**, 23, 40, 71
foundry, 39

fur trade, 25, 29, 45

geologist, 67
gold rush, 32, 46, 67, 71
government
    federal, 17, 31–33, 36–39, 41–43, 57, 62–63, 68
    local, 57, 68
    state, 57–61, **58**, 63, 67–68
    tribal, 57
Great Depression, 38–39, **38**, 71

Homestake Mine, 39, 67, 71, **71**
homesteads, 15, 33, **33**, 36, 46, 54

indigenous, 34
initiative, 58–59

Lakota (tribe), 9, 13–15, 25–26, 31, 33, 40–43, 45–46, 48, 51
Lead (town), 18, 32, 46, 52–53, 67, 69

Index

Lewis and Clark expedition, 5, 16–17, 29, **29**, 35, 43, 72

Louisiana Purchase, 28–29

massacre, 15, 33, 41, 43

Means, Russell, 41, 49

Missouri River, 8–9, 12–13, **12**, 16, 24–25, 29, 31, 35, 37, 39, 43, 65–67, 72–73, **73**

Mound Builders, 23–24, 43

museums, 15, 28, 34–35, 40, 52

Nakota (tribe), 25–26

Native Americans, 13, 20, 24–29, **24**, **26**, 31–33, **31**, 35, 41–43, **41**, **44**, 45–47, 49, 50–53, **51**

Oglala (tribe), 14, 27, 40, 42, 46, 48–49, 53

paleontological, 15

physics, 71

Pierre, 28, 35, 37, 43, 46, **56**, 57–58, 67

prairie dogs, 7, 13–14, 16–17, 21

Rapid City, 34, 39, 48, 51–52, 71

Red Cloud, 31–32, 45

referendum, 58–59, **59**, 60, **61**

refuge, 18

renewable energy, **12**, 39, 66–67, 69, 72

reservations, **18**, 27, 31–32, 40–43, **41**, 46–47, 49, **51**, 52–53, 57, 67

Rushmore, Mount, 7, 15, **36**, 37, 51, 69, 71

settlers, 16, 20, 26–27, 29, 31, 43, 45–47, 72

Sioux, 9, 13–15, **24**, 25–27, **26**, 31–33, 41–43, 45–46, 48–49, 55, 67
See also Dakota, Lakota, Nakota, Oglala

Sioux Falls, 8, 19, 34, 42, 47, 51, 66, 68

Sitting Bull, 31, **31**

spire, 12

tourism, 7, 14–16, 37, 51, 54, 60, 69, 71–73

unanimously, 63

University of South Dakota, 35, 40, 51

Vérendrye brothers, 25–26, 43

Vermillion, 35, 40, 51, 66

veto, 58, 60

Wilder, Laura Ingalls, 15, 49, 54

World War I, 37–38

World War II, 37, 39, 62

Wounded Knee, 15, 32–33, 41–43, 49